MICHAEL SOLOMONOV
STEVEN COOK

Easy, Essential, Delicious

Israeli Soul

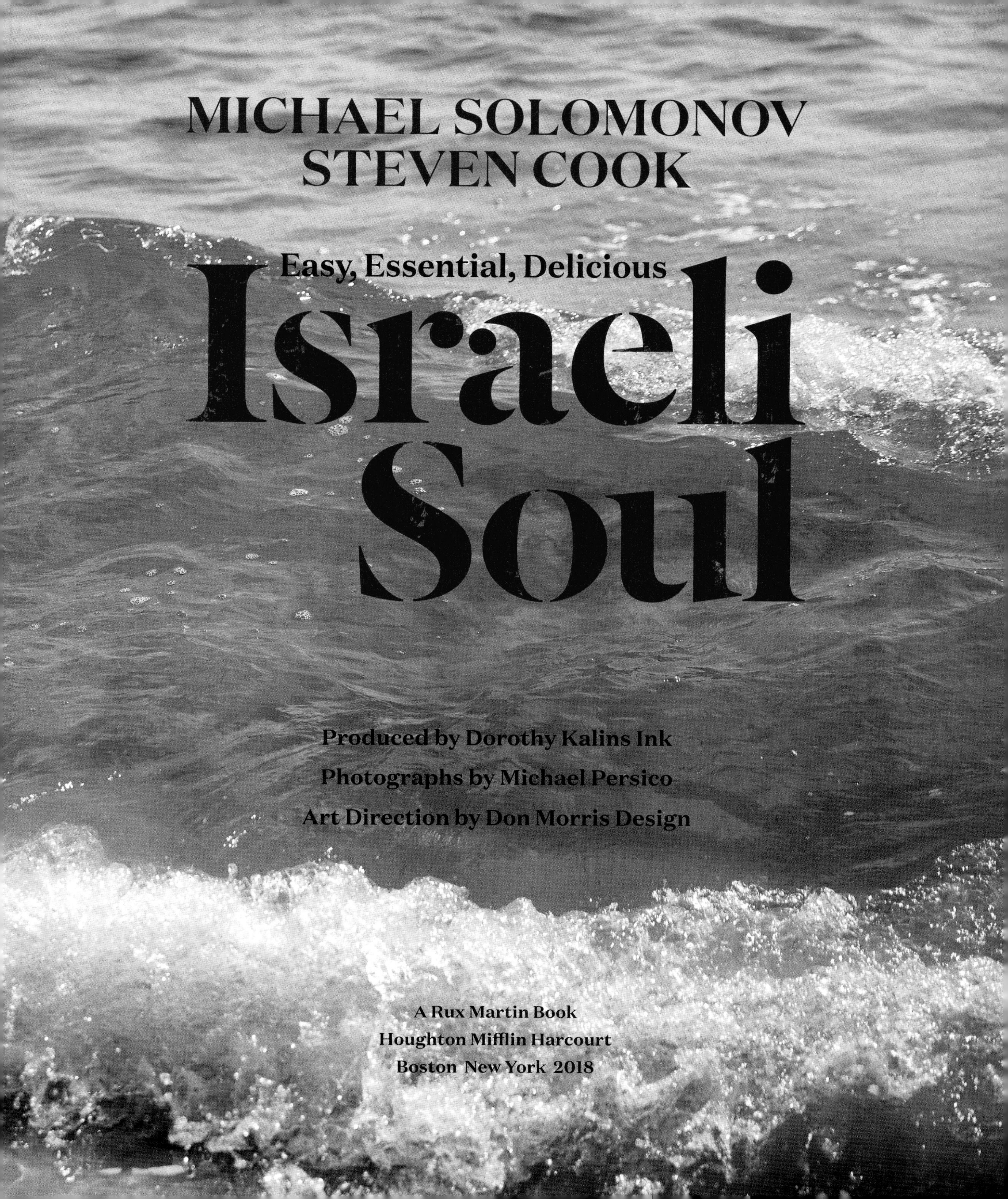

MICHAEL SOLOMONOV
STEVEN COOK

Easy, Essential, Delicious
Israeli Soul

Produced by Dorothy Kalins Ink

Photographs by Michael Persico

Art Direction by Don Morris Design

A Rux Martin Book
Houghton Mifflin Harcourt
Boston New York 2018

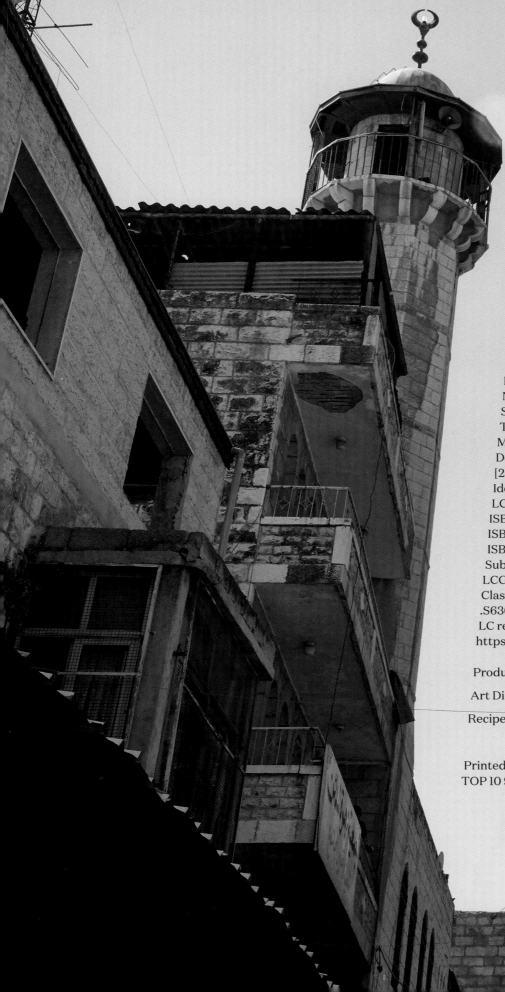

hmhco.com

Library of Congress Cataloging-in-Publication
Data:
Names: Solomonov, Michael, author. | Cook,
Steven (Restaurateur), author.
Title: Israeli soul : easy, essential, delicious /
Michael Solomonov, Steven Cook.
Description: Boston : Houghton Mifflin Harcourt,
[2018] | "A Rux Martin book."
Identifiers: LCCN 2018017712 (print) |
LCCN 2018021734 (ebook) |
ISBN 9780544971271 (ebook) |
ISBN 9780544970373 (paper over board) |
ISBN 9781328633453 (special ed)
Subjects: LCSH: Cooking, Israeli. | Kosher food. |
LCGFT: Cookbooks.
Classification: LCC TX724 (ebook) | LCC TX724
.S636 2018 (print) | DDC 641.595694—dc23
LC record available at
https://lccn.loc.gov/2018017712

Produced by Dorothy Kalins Ink, LLC

Art Direction by Don Morris Design

Recipe Editor: Peggy Paul Casella

Printed in China
TOP 10 9 8 7 6 5 4 3 2 1

To Evelyn Solomonov,
Susan Cook, and
Laurel Rudavsky

*"A mother understands
what a child does not say"*
—JEWISH PROVERB

Contents

IN THE HAND

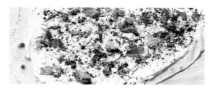

Contents

FROM THE BAKERY

FROM THE ICEBOX

Endpapers: Old City, Jerusalem: Muslim Quarter
Title pages: Ripe pomegranates, Galilee; the Mediterranean at Caesarea
Dedication: Jerusalem
Introduction: Hills of Galilee, Fishing at Akko
Map illustration by Don Morris

Acknowledgments: Juice seller, Tzfat
Last page: Olives at Haim Rafael, Tel Aviv
Endpapers: Ancient olive trees, Galilee

Introduction

By the time you read this, Israel will be seventy years old and Zahav, our Israeli restaurant in Philadelphia, will be ten. For ten years we've been calling Zahav a "modern Israeli restaurant," but that phrase has never felt particularly apt. After all, there's nothing modern about cooking pita in a wood-burning oven or kebabs over a charcoal grill.

And yet, Israel is a modern country, formed within the lifetime of some of its citizens. We've been puzzling our way through this contradiction for the last decade. There is a common misconception that Israeli food equals Middle Eastern food. But this is a vast oversimplification that obscures a remarkable story. The soul of Israeli cuisine lies in the journey these foods have taken to the ends of the earth and back, to be woven together in a nascent culture that is both ancient and modern.

It is not just the food of pre-Mandate Palestine, a cuisine that, in any case, was already familiar to the Jews of Iraq, Syria, and Lebanon. Nor is it simply the collected recipes of European, Balkan, and North African Jews returning to their ancestral homeland.

For two millennia, Jews have been wandering the earth, embracing the cultures and cuisines of their local hosts, adapting them to their religious and dietary needs, and transmitting the results at each stop along the way. The establishment of Israel in 1948 created a repository for all of these traditions—and a place for them to evolve in strange and wonderful ways.

For us, Israeli soul is sabich, the now classic sandwich of fried eggplant, hard-boiled egg, and the mango pickle amba that developed in Israel from the Sabbath breakfast traditions of Iraqi Jews. It is rugelach, the Ashkenazi pastry, here treated to the Arabic practice of saturating pastries in syrup. It is borekas, the stuffed savory pastries whose flaky dough made its way from Spain, through the Ottoman Empire to Bulgaria, and finally to Israel, where they are now a national obsession.

Like America, Israel is a product of migration. The vast majority of Israelis are only a few generations removed from a completely different life, in a completely different place. Food is a bridge that connects them to their heritage—and to each other.

What is the taste of home? Can the memory of childhood be captured in a single bite? How soulful and satisfying is the dish that made its way from the Diaspora to be reborn in Israel? There is a Hebrew expression, *l'dor v'dor*—literally "from generation to generation." It is the framework on which the survival of the Jewish people has been built for thousands of years, assuring that our values and traditions will outlive us. Our friend and farmer Mark Dornstreich (of blessed memory) used to say that it's impossible to be a first-generation farmer. It takes longer than a few years to establish a fruitful relationship with the land. Maybe it's the same with restaurants. A ten-year-old restaurant like Zahav is practically geriatric in America. In Israel, it is a toddler.

The parents of Rachel Arcovi, owner of the Hadera restaurant Opera, moved to Tel Aviv from Yemen in 1911. The family lived among immigrants from all over, and Rachel's mother learned to make Ashkenazi specialties like kugel, tzimmes, and gefilte fish, which she cooked alongside the Yemenite staples she had learned from her own mother. Her family moved north to Hadera in 1936, sustaining itself any way it could, often by working in orchards or packing plants. In 1974 Rachel took over Opera, a struggling coffee house, which continued to struggle. Her son and his friends, well aware of her gifts as a home cook, encouraged her to use those talents and expand the menu. Forty-three years later, Opera is an institution supporting three generations (and counting).

Opera's Yemenite soup is transformative—Rachel still eats it every day—but the money, she says, is in malawach, the flaky Yemenite fry bread. In 1988, the family opened a malawach factory, becoming the first to commercialize and help transform an immigrant dish into a food beloved by Israelis of every background. Eight of Rachel's eleven grandchildren now work at the restaurant or the factory. Last year the family opened a bakery, where they make all their own pita.

The theme of second- and third-generation owners is one we encountered again and again as we researched this book in Israel, returning to old favorites and discovering new ones. There is a dynastic quality to restaurants there,

a sense that proprietors are caretakers of traditions that must be preserved and passed down. Even with first-generation owners—like Rafi Guetta, whose Guetta is an homage to the Tripolitan cooking of his ancestors, or Arik Rosenthal of HaKosem, a fastidious temple of falafel and shawarma—we found an earnestness and respect for tradition, along with an understanding that this food would remain relevant only as long as it was delicious.

Such feelings were our guide in writing *Israeli Soul*. We have developed recipes that help tell the story of Israel. And we have taken special care to make them accessible and delicious. This is food that's meant to be cooked and meant to be shared.

L'dor v'dor.

Israeli Soul Odyssey

Tel Aviv

CARMEL MARKET

The Druze Corner, 1b HaCarmel

HaMalabiya, corner, 60 Allenby and 28 Gadera *(page 330)*

HaShomer, 1 HaShomer *(page 109)*

Mercaz HaBoreeka, 42 HaCarmel *(page 289)*

M25 Meatmarket, 30 Simtat HaCarmel *(page 276)*

LEVINSKY MARKET
en.shuktlv.co.il

Café Levinsky 41, 41 Levinsky *(page 353)*

Borekas Penso, 43 Levinsky *(page 320)*

Haim Rafael, 36 Levinsky *(page 217)*

Mati Bar, 84 Levinsky *(page 207)*

Etzel Tzion, 61 HaYarkon, corner Trumpeldor *(page 137)*

Guetta, 6 Yerushalaim Avenue, gueta-rest.co.il *(page 243)*

HaKosem, 1 Shlomo HaMelekh Street, falafelhakosem.com *(page 89)*

Itzik and Ruti, 53 Shenkin Street *(page 206)*

Mifgash HaOsher, 105 King George Street *(page 28)*

Sabich Tchernichovsky, 2 Tchernichovsky Street *(page 65)*

GIVATAYIM

Oved Sabich, 3–7 Sirkin Street *(page 83)*

Jaffa

Abu Hassan, 1 Dolphin Street *(page 143)*

Haj Kahil, 18 David Raziel Street, hajkahil.rest-e.co.il *(page 99)*

Itzik HaGadol, 3 David Raziel Street *(page 179)*

Lod

Abu Michel, 29 Sderot Tsahai *(pages 148–149)*

Jerusalem

MACHANE YEHUDA MARKET
Agrippas Street, en.machne.co.il

Aricha Sabich, 83 Agrippas Street *(page 67)*

Azura, 4 HaEshkol Street *(pages 228–241)*

Borekas Ramle, 44 Agrippas Street *(page 311)*

Hatzot, 121 Agrippas Street, hatzot.co.il *(pages 122–125)*

Khachapuria, 5 HaShikma Street *(page 290)*

Morris Restaurant, corner, HaCharuv and HaTut Streets *(page 273)*

Bandora Shawarma, 36 Yafo Street *(page 106)*

Helman Bakery, 18 Natan Strauss Street *(page 327)*

Falafel Uzi, Yeshayahu *(pages 28–29)*

Hummus Ben Sira, 4 Ben Sira Street *(page 23)*

OLD CITY

Jewish Quarter

Muslim Quarter

Zalatimo's, Christian Quarter, *(page 334)*

Akko

Endomela, HaHagana Street *(page 364)*

Hummus El Abed Abu Hamid, Old Akko Lighthouse *(page 169)*

Kashash, Binyamin MiTudela, Turkish Market *(pages 324–326)*

Shamsa, covered market, *(page 87)*

Ein al-Assad

Al Ein *(page 87)*

Hadera

Opera, 61 HaNassi Street *(page 235)*

Haifa

Maayan haBira, 4 Natanzon Street *(page 208)*

Yonak, 23 Kibuts Galuyot *(page 213)*

Hod HaSharon

Kaduri Falafel, 59 Ramatayim Road *(page 217)*

Sabich HaSharon, 68 Nahalat Binyamin *(page 81)*

Kfar Saba

Gohar, 26 HaTa'as Street *(page 246)*

Penguin, 43 Rothchild *(page 367)*

Tiferet, 147 Rehov Weizmann *(page 22)*

Karkur

D'Vora Falafel, 30 Hameyasdim *(pages 38–39)*

Maalot Tarshiha

Buza Ice Cream, 1 HaShuk Street *(page 364)*

Ramla

Halil, 6 Kehilat Detroit Street *(page 159)*

Umm al-Fahm

Restaurant El Babour, Highway 65 *(page 275)*

Tzfat

Fricassee Zahava, 26 Yerushalayim Street *(pages 286–289)*

Philadelphia

Abe Fisher, 1623 Sansom Street *(page 207)*

Dizengoff, 1625 Sansom Street *(page 140)*

Federal Donuts, 1632 Sansom *(page 346)*

Goldie, 1526 Sansom Street *(page 44)*

K'far Bakery, 1218 Sansom Street *(page 310)*

Rooster Soup, 1526 Sansom Street *(page 44)*

Zahav, 237 St. James Place *(page 20)*

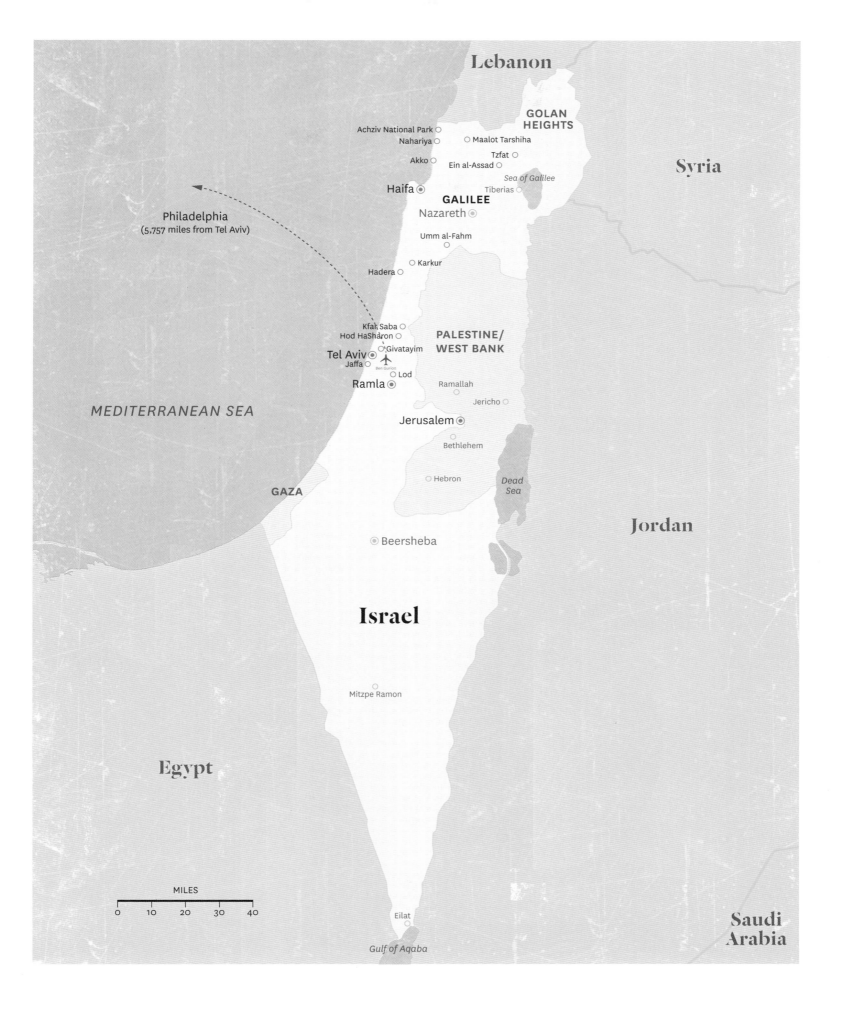

Lebanon

GOLAN
HEIGHTS

Syria

Achziv National Park ○
Nahariya ○   ○ Maalot Tarshiha
Akko ○   Tzfat ○
Ein al-Assad ○
Sea of Galilee

Haifa ◉   ○ Tiberias
GALILEE
Nazareth ◉

Umm al-Fahm ○

○ Karkur
Hadera ○

Philadelphia
(5,757 miles from Tel Aviv)

Kfar Saba ○
Hod HaSharon ○   PALESTINE/
○ Givatayim   WEST BANK
Tel Aviv ◉
Jaffa ○   Ben Gurion ✈
○ Lod
Ramla ◉   ○ Ramallah
○ Jericho

Jerusalem ◉

MEDITERRANEAN SEA   Bethlehem ○

○ Hebron   Dead
Sea
GAZA

Jordan

Beersheba ◉

Israel

Egypt

Mitzpe Ramon ○

MILES

0   10   20   30   40

Eilat ○   Saudi
Arabia
Gulf of Aqaba

While most of us don't have daily access to this bounty at Tel Aviv's Carmel Market, it's become easier to find excellent ingredients at home.

Resources

We recognize that there are spices and sauces and other preparations in this book that might seem unfamiliar to you. Yet we hope you'll never be put off from trying a recipe for want of an ingredient.

Whenever you encounter something that's not in your pantry, know that, first of all, we encourage substitutions. For example, we specify Aleppo pepper in many recipes. Don't have that? No worries. Substitute a combination of sweet paprika, red pepper flakes, and a pinch of cayenne. We heartily recommend making a jar of hawaij, a blend of the Yemenite Holy Trinity—ground turmeric, black pepper, and ground cumin—and using it to flavor everything from chicken soup to scrambled eggs. For the pickled shipka peppers *(page 137)*, feel free to use pickled jalapeños. There's an entire chapter on Druze mountain bread, but in a pinch, substitute handmade flour tortillas.

We're all in favor of bottled sauces, especially when just a spoonful or two is called for in a recipe. Take the pickled mango sauce amba. Excellent versions are available in jars (we even sell them at our falafel shop, Goldie). But we also give you a recipe for making Classic Mango Amba from scratch *(page 79)*, which is itself a delightful experience. Similarly, Israeli cuisine loves its hot sauces—harifs. Bottles of the good stuff abound. Same for harissa, the North African red pepper sauce. Great ones come in jars. Yet with the recipes on pages 150 to 151, you can discover how to make your own spice blends and sauces, or even ferment your own hot sauce.

And while we encourage you to discover and get to know the spice shops and Middle Eastern markets available to you, we do want to share our favorite sources.

Our friend chef Lior Lev Sercarz is a master spice blender. His website, **laboiteny.com**, will lead you to a magical assortment of the freshly ground and pungent spices we use frequently. It's a trip to visit his New York City store at 724 Eleventh Avenue.

Kalustyans.com is another favorite source for spices and jarred condiments, plus a mind-boggling selection of other ingredients like grains, teas, and nuts. This website never disappoints. We also highly recommend wandering the fragrant aisles at their shop at 123 Lexington Avenue in New York City.

We are big fans of Soom tahini, made in Israel from Ethiopian sesame seeds and imported by three American sisters, as a base for our Quick Tehina Sauce *(page 145)*. To order, check out their website, **soomfoods.com**. Note: When we refer to sesame paste, we use the Hebrew word *tehina*, which is the same as tahini.

Increasingly, grocery chains like Whole Foods and Trader Joe's are stocking excellent tahini, organic canned chickpeas, fresh turmeric root, and spices worth trying.

We became so fond of the way our food at Rooster Soup looks on the enamelware bowls, plates, and platters from Crow Canyon Home, **crowcanyonhome.com**, that we used their pieces to photograph the recipes in this book.

You can order almost anything, of course, on **amazon.com**.

A note on Hebrew phonetics:
As Mike puts it, "In Israel, every English spelling is different!" After consulting many sources, we have chosen our versions for consistency. When searching Google, you'll find, as we did, that each search yields a different result. Take one of our favorite restaurants in Tel Aviv, Arik Rosenthal's HaKosem, which means "The Magician." We have seen it spelled as one word, Hakosem, or with a lowercase "h," haKosem, or, as we choose to refer to it, HaKosem. Even town names vary in their spelling. You could be going to ancient Akko, on the northern Mediterranean coast, or Acre, its Arabic spelling. Is it Ramla or Ramle? Heading for the mystical town of Tzfat, you will see signs for Safed, Zefat, Tsfat, Zfat, Safad, and Safet. They all lead to the same place.

IN THE HAND

CHAPTER 1

Falafel

"Is falafel Israeli? Are Israelis Middle Eastern?"

For people trying to understand Israeli cuisine, falafel is a conundrum, because it is both demonstrably Israeli and not Israeli. A decade ago, when we were trying to raise money for Zahav, our modern Israeli restaurant, investors would ask, heads nodding: "So . . . like, falafel and stuff?" When the restaurant finally opened, we heard about falafel again, from our guests: "What, no falafel?"

Falafel, fried balls of ground chickpeas, may be the unofficial national dish of Israel, but it didn't originate there, and we were loath to reinforce a misleading stereotype that Israelis eat falafel three times a day. (By the way, the other unofficial national dish of Israel is p'tcha, or jellied calves' feet, also not on the menu at Zahav.) And yet we know that Israelis eat falafel by the truckload. So is it Israeli? Like many other foods of the region, falafel has defied geographical borders.

Legend holds that as early as the fourth century, Coptic Christians in Egypt ate fava bean falafel on Fridays as a Lenten replacement for meat. But there are no references to this Egyptian ta'amiyeh, or its chickpea-based cousin, in Egyptian literature until the late nineteenth century. And other signs point to the proliferation of falafel as a modern phenomenon, including the advanced baking technology that commercialized pita bread, as well as the idea that oil would have been too expensive to use for deep-frying until modern times. These arguments, put forth by Hebrew University professor Shaul Stampfer, present a more nuanced view of falafel's popularity.

Previous spread: The bounty at Tiferet, a Kfar Saba falafel stand. *This page:* For decades, my go-to falafel has been from D'Vora *(page 26)* in Karkur, north of Tel Aviv.

Tiferet

KFAR SABA | Also known as "the falafel by the bus stop," the name roughly translates to "the luxuriousness of falafel." Tiferet is a classic example of the "toppings bar" falafel shop model. For 18 shekels (about $5), you can stuff your pita or laffa with as many pickles, vegetables, French fries, herbs, and sauces as you can cram in.

Falafel certainly predates Jewish settlement in pre-Independence Israel. It has long been served on platters—alongside hummus and other mezze, for example—throughout the Levant, possibly for centuries. Some contend that legume fritters were an innovation from the Indian subcontinent. But the late, great Jewish food historian Gil Marks credits Yemenite Jewish immigrants with putting it all together in a pita sandwich around 1948, the time of Israeli Independence.

The idea of falafel in Israel is not such a great leap, since throughout history nomadic Jews have adapted the local foods of their host countries. When Eastern European Jews began arriving in Palestine, they were eager to shed the formal constraints of the old country. These pioneers enthusiastically embraced falafel because it represented the opposite of their previous way of life. This was the food of the people, exotically spiced, vibrant with fresh vegetables and tehina, and eaten on the street, not in the formality of a dining room. The falafel sandwich quickly became a symbol of the rugged, self-reliant Israeli pioneer and contributed to the establishment of a national identity.

In 2017, we finally caved and opened our own falafel shop called Goldie, a little spot just down the street from Dizengoff, the hummus restaurant that we opened in 2014. In true Israeli fashion, we run fresh-baked pita from Dizengoff to Goldie throughout the day. We treat Goldie like an Israeli burger joint, serving only falafel, French fries, and tehina shakes. It just happens to be vegan.

Like pizza and ramen, falafel is now a global phenomenon. I've eaten it in Los Angeles, Paris, and Costa Rica. Does anyone care that in Japan they eat pizza topped with corn and mayonnaise? So back to the original question: Is falafel Israeli? Yes. And no. And does it matter?

Hummus Ben Sira

JERUSALEM | A small and crowded hummusiya in the Mamilla neighborhood of Jerusalem, Ben Sira also makes incredibly light falafel. Eat some alongside a bowl of sweet and rich Jerusalem-style hummus, typically topped with sautéed spiced ground beef and chickpeas.

The noble, if graffitied, profile of old Jaffa (or Yafo or Yaffo) never ceases to make our hearts beat faster as we round the coast south of Tel Aviv.

Falafel Is Where Your Heart Is

It was my junior year of high school, and my family had just moved back to Israel, where I was promptly shipped off to a boarding school for troubled Israeli youth and foreigners. On the day of parent-teacher conferences, I watched as my parents huddled with Rena and Ruvane, the school's directors, to discuss my performance.

From my father's animated hand motions and his grave expression, it looked to me like I might be getting kicked out of school. Turned out those gestures meant directions to the nearby **D'Vora Falafel**. He'd heard it was good.

Until that point, falafel was, to me, the boxed Osem mix my mother would break out on Yom Ha'atzmaut (Israeli Independence Day). Just add water and fry into dense balls overpowered by spice. I wasn't into sauce or vegetables or much else at that age, nor was I into dry falafel balls stuffed into an even drier supermarket pita.

At first sight, I could tell that D'Vora Falafel was completely different. I was mesmerized as I watched the counterman build each sandwich with the practiced economy of motion of someone who's been doing it for a long time (twenty-five years at last count). His hands worked together like trapeze artists. The left hand held the pita, top split open, applying just enough pressure to enlarge its wide mouth as his right hand scooped and flipped the ingredients—tehina, chopped tomatoes,

cabbage, falafel balls (fried to order)—up and into the pita with a spoon, his left thumb extended up to catch and guide each ingredient into the perfect spot inside.

I've been saying D'Vora is the best falafel in Israel for more than a decade now, and I return every chance I get. But I've come to realize that the search for the greatest falafel on earth—something of a national obsession in Israel—is ultimately pointless. Almost all falafel in Israel is very good. Its greatness depends as much on who's eating it as on its quality. And everyone knows where to get the best.

"These are not falafel! These are balls of gold!" shouts the falafel vendor in the public market in Akko, in Hebrew and English. His confidence and conviction are admittedly traits not typically in short supply among Israeli men. But his falafel were, indeed, excellent.

Kaduri Falafel

HOD HaSHARON |
Occupying less than 50
square feet of kiosk built
right on the sidewalk of
the main road through
Hod HaSharon, Kaduri
makes the best falafel
per square foot in Israel.
On our last visit, the
owner proudly showed
us a clipping from an
American magazine that
called Kaduri one of
Israel's top falafel joints.
As it turned out, I wrote
the article.

"These are not falafel, these are balls of gold," shouts a falafel maker in old Akko.

Mifgash HaOsher

TEL AVIV | Bentzi Arbel takes a minimalist approach to falafel at his aptly named "Happiness Joint" on King George Street in Tel Aviv. A chef who worked in some of Tel Aviv's best kitchens, Bentzi became disillusioned with the seriousness and intensity of high-end restaurants. Instead, he wanted to find the happiness that he remembered as a child, eating falafel with his father at Orion, in Haifa.

Bentzi believes that herbs are not good for you when exposed to high temperatures, so his superlight falafel are a pure expression of chickpeas, fresh vegetables, tehina, and joy. It's not surprising that Mifgash HaOsher has already developed a loyal following.

At **Mifgash HaOsher** ("Happiness Joint") in Tel Aviv, Bentzi Arbel and his partner, Omri Kravitz, both classically trained chefs, talk falafel-osophy and the joys of returning to cooking simple, perfect food. Bentzi's falafel are pure: just chickpeas, water, and salt. No spices, herbs, garlic, or even a pinch of baking powder to lighten them. But they're neither dense nor bland; they're light and fluffy, and the beautiful pale caramel color of Tater Tots. The shop itself is an altar to simplicity, and if you told me this was the best falafel sandwich in Israel—layered with chopped cucumbers, tomatoes, and tehina—you'd get no argument.

Yehuda Sichel, the chef-owner of Abe Fisher, our Philadelphia restaurant focusing on Ashkenazi Jewish cuisine, might dissent, however. His heart belongs to **Falafel Uzi**, a small shop in Zichron Moshe, between downtown Jerusalem and the ultra-orthodox Mea Shearim neighborhood. When Yehuda lived in Jerusalem, this was his neighborhood falafel joint—the owner, Uzi (of course), still remembers him more than a decade later. Buses frequently stop at the traffic light in front of the shop, and Yehuda would be pressed into service, ferrying fresh falafel sandwiches to the drivers, like the fictional gyro stand on the New York City subway platform on *Seinfeld*.

The falafel at Uzi is very, very good. But to Yehuda, it is the best because it tastes like a particularly momentous period of his life. D'Vora is the same for me. It tastes like the beginning of my love affair with Israel.

Falafel Uzi

JERUSALEM | Uzi and his son Chaim have run this popular falafel shop since long before our partner, chef Yehuda Sichel, frequented it as a teenage troublemaker in Jerusalem. Bus drivers like to block traffic out front and honk their horns, prompting Uzi to enlist the nearest customer to deliver a sandwich and collect payment.

Goldie Falafel

Makes about 30 pieces (enough for 5 or 6 sandwiches)

1 tablespoon baking powder

1 tablespoon kosher salt

2 teaspoons ground cumin

2 teaspoons ground turmeric

1 pound dried chickpeas, soaked in water overnight and drained

Big handful fresh parsley

Big handful fresh cilantro

1 medium carrot, peeled and chopped

1 small onion, chopped

4 garlic cloves

2 tablespoons cold water, plus more as needed

Canola oil, for frying

Based on the master recipe we developed for Goldie, this version is not too spicy and lets the subtle chickpea taste come through. Herbs and vegetables help keep the falafel balls moist; pulsing in a food processor creates the crispy exterior.

1. Mix together the baking powder, salt, cumin, and turmeric in a small bowl.

2. Layer half the ingredients in a food processor in this order: chickpeas, fresh herbs, vegetables, garlic, and the mixed dry seasonings. Repeat with the remaining ingredients in the same order. Add the water and pulse until very finely chopped and the mixture holds together when pinched between two fingers. If necessary, add a bit more water and pulse again to get the right consistency.

3. Scoop the batter into a colander set over a large bowl to drain while you make the balls. Squeeze out the liquid from the batter with your hands until the dough stays together, then shape into 1-inch balls. Set the balls aside on a plate.

4. Heat a couple of inches of canola oil to 350°F in a large pot. Lower the balls into the hot oil with a long-handled slotted spoon and raise the heat to high to maintain the temperature of the oil. Fry in batches for 3 to 4 minutes, or until the falafel balls are brown and crispy (but not burnt!).

5. Immediately transfer the falafel with a slotted spoon to a paper towel–lined plate to drain. Serve hot.

6. Make your sandwich by layering 2 falafel balls with salad (page 45) and sauce (page 35) in a pita, and repeating till the pita is full.

Falalel Cart

HADERA | This mobile cart is next to a school in the neighborhood of Givat Olga (lines are long when school's in session). They also make boreeka, the fried Tunisian brik pastry stuffed with potato and egg.

CILANTRO ONION CHICKPEAS

CUMIN TURMERIC GARLIC PARSLEY CARROTS

A. Layer half the ingredients in the bowl of a food processor in the right order.

B. Repeat with the remaining ingredients, layered in the same order.

C. Add the water and process until the entire mixture is very finely chopped.

D. Add a bit more water if needed to make sure the mixture holds together.

E. Drain the mixture, squeeze out the liquid, and, with your hands, form 1-inch balls.

F. Fry the balls for 3 to 4 minutes in a few inches of oil heated to 350°F, until the balls are brown and crispy.

Tehina Variations

Tehina and falafel go together like hummus and pita. Pure tehina, with its slightly bitter brashness, is the perfect partner for the mild fried falafel balls. But other bold additions can elevate a falafel: the fresh green chiles of the quickly made green condiment schug; the smokier dried chile heat of harissa; or the fruity, fermented flavors of amba. We created these flavored sauces, based on our Quick Tehina Sauce, to customize your falafel.

Tehina Ketchup
Makes 1 heaping cup

Ketchup is the perfect balance of sweet, salty, sour, and savory. We didn't think it could be improved upon until we added the rich bitterness of tehina, the funkiness of amba, and the earthy heat of harissa. Wow! Works on absolutely everything, especially Goldie French Fries *(page 46)*.

- 1 **cup ketchup**
- 1½ **tablespoons Quick Tehina Sauce** *(page 145)*
- 1½ **teaspoons Classic Mango Amba** *(page 79)* **or store-bought**
- 1 **teaspoon Fresh Harissa** *(page 150)* **or store-bought**

Mix together all of the ingredients in a small bowl. Refrigerate in a covered container for up to a week.

Schug Tehina
Makes 1 heaping cup

- 1 **cup Quick Tehina Sauce** *(page 145)*
- 1 **tablespoon Everyday Schug** *(page 151)* **or store-bought**
- **Kosher salt**
- **Lemon juice**

Mix together the tehina sauce and schug in a small bowl. Taste and add salt and a squeeze of lemon juice as needed. Refrigerate in a covered container for up to a week.

Harissa Tehina
Makes 1 heaping cup

- 1 **cup Quick Tehina Sauce** *(page 145)*
- 1 **tablespoon Fresh Harissa** *(page 150)* **or store-bought**
- **Kosher salt**
- **Lemon juice**

Mix together the tehina sauce and harissa in a small bowl. Taste and add salt and a squeeze of lemon juice as needed. Refrigerate in a covered container for up to a week.

Amba Tehina
Makes 1 cup

- ½ **cup Quick Tehina Sauce** *(page 145)*
- ½ **cup Classic Mango Amba** *(page 79)* **or store-bought**
- **Kosher salt**
- **Lemon juice**

Mix together the tehina sauce and amba in a small bowl. Taste and add salt and a squeeze of lemon juice as needed. Refrigerate in a covered container for up to a week.

Everyday dream meal: fresh falafel stuffed into pitas, with Israeli salad, red cabbage, and a choice of amba, schug, or harissa tehina *(page 35).*

It's Always Lunchtime Somewhere

We're standing in the middle of the rambling compound that makes up **D'Vora Falafel**. Chava Visish, the second-generation owner, operates the falafel machine with her left hand, a cigarette dangling from the corner of her mouth. With her right hand, she shows us why D'Vora's pita is so good: She takes one and balls it up tightly in her fist, then she opens her palm, and we watch as the pita springs back into its original shape. She looks up at us expectantly, wanting to make sure we understand the gravity of what has happened—as though she had just revealed how to produce nuclear energy by squeezing together atoms in her hand.

Most falafel shops (and restaurants for that matter) don't make their own pita, but D'Vora bakes six hundred loaves a day at its bakery up the road. The walls of the pita are thick and fluffy; the interiors have the nooks and crannies of an English muffin. Visible strands of gluten give the pita the elasticity it needs to contain a sandwich that is as complete and harmonious as any we've eaten.

This exemplary pita elevates D'Vora's falafel sandwich above its simple components. And it's a big part of what makes the shop, an hour north of Tel Aviv, in the middle of nowhere, a destination—no small feat considering you can't turn around in Israel without ending up in line at a falafel place. Chava's mother, D'Vora, emigrated from Yemen just before Independence and opened the falafel stand in 1966. So many falafel shops in Israel are owned by Yemenites that you would be forgiven for thinking that falafel has roots in Yemen.

The truer reason is that restaurant work everywhere attracts poor immigrants, who are willing to work hard. And no one was poorer than the Yemenite Jews who arrived in Israel around the time of Independence. In the same way that Greeks came to dominate the diner business in America, Yemenite newcomers saw falafel as a path to upward mobility.

The barriers to entry in restaurants are low to begin with, and a falafel stand requires little more than a fryer. Often mentioned in the conversation about Israel's best falafel, **Kaduri Falafel**, on the main road in Hod HaSharon, north of Tel Aviv, occupies a freestanding building

that takes up less than fifty square feet. From this tiny footprint, falafel has sustained multiple generations of the stand's two founding families.

D'Vora first opened in 1966, a period when unemployment in the region hovered around 50 percent. An economic boom followed the Six-Day War in 1967, and the stand has grown more popular every year since. It's amazing what zero marketing can do. Even though it's right on the main road, D'Vora can be difficult to find. The stand is somewhat hidden from passing cars, and there's really nowhere to park anyway. It makes you wonder if this is intentional, as if the proprietors want to make sure you're properly motivated to be there.

D'Vora Falafel

KARKUR | Even at three in the afternoon on a weekday, there's still a line at D'Vora. The crowd includes an IDF soldier, machine gun dangling off his hip; an Arab family with two little girls; and a table of well-dressed middle-class women. The construction workers' overstuffed pitas are already half-eaten in the short walk between the window and the picnic tables in the courtyard.

Fresh Green Garbanzo Falafel

Makes about 30 pieces (enough for 5 or 6 sandwiches)

When springtime rolls around, we love to feature the bright, vegetal flavor of fresh green chickpeas before they are dried.

Combine 6 ounces dried chickpeas, soaked overnight and drained, with 10 ounces shucked fresh green chickpeas (available in spring at specialty markets and online). Using the same measurements for the other ingredients, make the batter as shown in Goldie Falafel *(page 30)*. Scrape the batter into a bowl. This batter is wetter and won't hold together as well, so add a bit of chickpea flour or other flour a little at a time until the batter holds together enough to make balls.

VARIATION

English Pea Falafel

Makes about 30 pieces (enough for 5 or 6 sandwiches)

You can make falafel with almost any legume, fresh or dried. English peas are as sweet as candy in the summer and make a delightful change of pace. They're great with a yogurt-based dipping sauce.

Combine 6 ounces dried chickpeas, soaked overnight and drained, with 10 ounces fresh green peas. Using the same measurements for the other ingredients, make the batter as shown in Goldie Falafel *(page 30)*. Scrape the batter into a bowl. This batter is wetter, so add a bit of chickpea flour or other flour a little at a time until the batter holds together enough to form balls.

A Balance in Every Bite

When I was young, my father owned a couple of Subway sandwich franchises in Pittsburgh. The company refers to its employees as "Sandwich Artists," which always makes me giggle a little. Sandwiches are simple food: Slap two pieces of bread around whatever you find in the fridge and call it lunch. Now that I'm in the sandwich business myself, I've come to realize that there's a whole lot more to it than that. A great sandwich requires balancing each element—richness, texture, acidity, salt, spice—in every bite.

Building falafel is an even bigger challenge, because you load the pita from the bottom up and eat it from the top down. This is why I've always been puzzled by the falafel shop toppings bar where they give you your pita filled with the fried balls and then you confront a self-service counter and proceed to cram a bunch of salads, pickles, and condiments on top.

But a toppings bar does have its charms. For 18 shekels (the equivalent of $5) at **Tiferet Ha'Falafel**, the beloved stand by the bus station near where my mom lived, north of Tel Aviv, in Kfar Saba, you basically have access to an all-you-can-eat buffet of salads, pickles, French fries, and condiments. But for me, the beauty of any great sandwich (and especially falafel) rests in its simplicity and harmony. "The best hamburger is just plain meat with salt and pepper," says D'Vora's Chava Visish. Accordingly, at D'Vora your choices are essentially limited to whether you want your falafel spicy and what you'll drink with it.

At our falafel shop, **Goldie**, in Philadelphia, the "no toppings bar" ethos has been a part of our philosophy since day one. We build each sandwich to your specifications with our (modestly) practiced hands. And it tastes like a work of art, if we do say so ourselves!

Caitlin McMillan, Goldie

PHILADELPHIA | Chef Caitlin is the genius behind Goldie, the falafel shop we swore we would never open (but did anyway, on April Fool's Day, 2017). It's right upstairs from Rooster Soup, our luncheonette that supports the Broad Street Ministry's Hospitality Collaborative.

In addition to falafel sandwiches professionally constructed to your specifications (à la D'Vora, *page 26*, our "gold" standard for all things falafel), Goldie serves house-cut French fries and flavored milkshakes made with a tehina base. In our minds, the whole operation resembles a vegan, kosher, Middle Eastern burger joint.

Salad Variations

Before pita and falafel became best friends and professional collaborators, falafel had a long and distinguished career, not just packed into a sandwich but as a crunchy salad—a standalone mezze. Like most fried foods, falafel does well accompanied by a tangy dipping sauce and a generous shake of za'atar *(below right)*. Here are variations on the usual suspects.

Green Garbanzo Falafel with Labneh and Pomegranate

If you're lucky enough to find green garbanzos in season, these bright falafel shine on a base of labneh, fresh herbs, and pomegranate seeds.

English Pea Falafel with Herbed Tehina

Perched on a tehina- or yogurt-based sauce, richly scattered with fresh green herbs: think parsley, cilantro, basil, chives.

Goldie Falafel with Herbs and Israeli Salad

A perfect poem of crunch and green, Goldie Salad celebrates delicately spiced falafel balls with leaves of mint and dill, chunks of cucumber and tomato, a swirl of tehina sauce, and plenty of za'atar. Toss with vinaigrette and top with falafel.

FALAFEL SALAD VINAIGRETTE: Whisk together 1 minced shallot and ¼ cup each fresh lemon juice, white wine vinegar, and date molasses in a small bowl. Slowly whisk in 1½ cups canola oil to emulsify the dressing. Taste and add kosher salt. Refrigerated, the dressing will keep for 1 week. Makes 2 cups.

Goldie French Fries

Serves 4

2 quarts cold water

⅔ cup apple cider vinegar

½ cup plus 1 tablespoon kosher salt

4 pounds Kennebec, russet, or Yukon Gold potatoes

Canola oil, for frying

Big pinch of any Shawarma Spice Blend *(page 150)*

Tehina Ketchup *(page 35)*, **for dipping**

The best French fries are fried two, sometimes even three, times. But when we were planning Goldie, we wanted a great French fry without all that extra frying. Our potatoes are briefly brined and steamed until just cooked through. After that, they spend the night uncovered in the freezer to let their exteriors dehydrate a bit. Then they need just a single dunk in the fryer for a French fry that seems to get crispier as it cools.

1. Make a brine in a large bowl with the water, vinegar, and salt. Whisk until the salt is fully dissolved.

2. Cut the potatoes lengthwise into ½-inch-thick slices, then cut the slices into sticks of equal width. Transfer the cut potatoes to the brine and let them soak for 1 hour at room temperature.

3. Bring an inch or two of water to a boil in a large pot and set a colander or large steamer basket inside the pot, making sure the bottom sits above the water. Use a slotted spoon to transfer the soaked potatoes to the steamer. Steam for about 20 minutes, or until the potatoes are just barely tender.

4. Remove the steamer basket from the heat, shake off any extra moisture, and spread the potatoes in a single layer on a baking sheet. Freeze uncovered for at least 12 hours.

5. To fry the potatoes, heat 1½ to 2 inches of canola oil to 350°F in a large pot. Using a long-handled slotted spoon, carefully lower the potatoes into the hot oil and turn the heat up to high to maintain the oil temperature. Fry the potatoes for 6 to 8 minutes, or until they are golden brown and crispy. When they're done, use the slotted spoon to transfer the fries to a paper towel–lined plate. Let them drain for a minute or two, then transfer to a large bowl, sprinkle with the Shawarma Spice Blend, and toss well. Serve with Tehina Ketchup.

A. Cut potatoes into ½-inch-thick slices, then cut the slices into equal-size fries.

B. Transfer the cut potatoes to the bowl of brine: cold water, vinegar, and salt. Soak for 1 hour.

C. Steam the brined potatoes in a colander over boiling water for about 20 minutes.

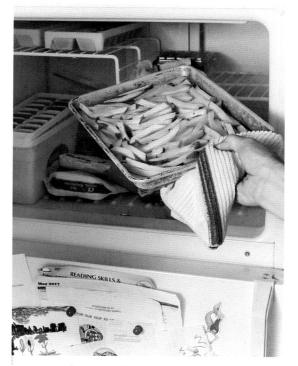

D. Freeze the steamed cut potatoes on a baking sheet for at least 12 hours.

E. In a deep pot, heat the oil to 350°F and lower in the frozen potatoes with a slotted spoon.

F. Fry the potatoes for 6 to 8 minutes, or until they are golden brown and crispy.

G. Lift the potatoes from the oil with the slotted spoon and drain on paper towels for a minute.

H. Sprinkle the fried potatoes with Shawarma Spice Blend *(page 150)*.

I. Vigorously toss the fried potatoes with the spice blend to distribute it evenly.

IN THE HAND

CHAPTER 2

Pita Bread

"Pita gives you two things: portablilty and the epiphany of the perfect bite."

There's so much to recommend baking bread at home that it's a shame we don't do it much anymore. For most of human history, making the daily bread was a sacred responsibility. But in the developed world, at least, bread is now such a factory-made, shelf-stable commodity that most of us buy our loaves a week at a time. We bake thousands of loaves of pita every day to supply our restaurants Dizengoff and Goldie. Although machines help us mix and portion the dough, each pita is rolled and baked by hand. Standing in front of a wood-burning oven all day long might sound tedious, but it's exactly where I want to be.

I love watching bakers scoop the dough balls onto the board, dust them with flour, and roll them into near-perfect circles with a few practiced motions of the wooden pin. They load the disks one by one onto the peel and gently slide them onto a vacant spot in the oven's blazing hearth. All of this while managing another half-dozen loaves already in the oven, rising and falling like dancing fountains.

That the artisanal bread movement is gaining steam is heartening, not the least because it connects us to a time when the bakery occupied a sanctified place in our daily lives. Nothing beats the satisfaction of baking pita at home. Nothing compares to the feel of the dough in your hands when

Previous spread: Making pita in my home kitchen seemed nuts, but then I figured it out. Piece of cake.

An impressive pita-making machine turns out perfect golden rounds in the heart of Machane Yehuda in Jerusalem. *At right*: Just one of the many busy bread sellers in the market.

it is just right, or the ancient smell of yeast and toasted wheat filling your house.

But for many of us, the very idea of making bread in our own kitchen is enough to send us running for the door. There's flour everywhere. The sink is full of bowls and utensils coated in sticky dough. The yeast may or may not answer our prayers. There has to be a better way!

With our recipe, you'll be pulling fresh, puffy pita out of the oven in about an hour. Using just your food processor, the dough is measured and mixed in under two minutes, so cleanup is a breeze. In fact, most of the hour involves waiting for the dough to rise, giving you time to balance your checkbook, get a massage, or change your profile status from tense to tranquil.

Pita Bread

Makes 4

2¼ cups all-purpose flour
1 (¼-ounce) packet active dry yeast
2 teaspoons kosher salt
1¼ teaspoons sugar
1 cup plus 3 tablespoons warm water
2 tablespoons olive oil

1. Combine the flour, yeast, salt, sugar, 1 cup of the water, and the olive oil in a food processor. Pulse just until a ball forms. With the machine running, stream in the remaining 3 tablespoons water and process for 1 minute. The dough should be loose and sticky. Scoop the dough into a large bowl and cover with a kitchen towel. Let rise at room temperature for 30 to 45 minutes, or until doubled in volume.

2. Place a baking stone or upside-down baking sheet on a rack in the bottom third of the oven and preheat the oven to 500°F (or as high as it will go).

3. Once the dough has finished rising, transfer to the refrigerator and let rest for at least 15 minutes or up to 3 hours. Remove and scrape the dough onto a lightly floured board. Pat it into a log shape, then cut it into 4 equal pieces, using just enough flour to keep it from sticking. Form each piece into a round by gently tucking the edges underneath, making sure to smooth the top. Transfer the whole board to the refrigerator for at least 10 minutes or up to 2 hours to relax the dough.

4. Remove the dough from the refrigerator and use a rolling pin or the palm of your hand to gently flatten each round into a 4- to 6-inch disk. The dough will be sticky, but resist the urge to douse it in flour. The less you prod it or weigh it down, the better. The key is to not roll or flatten the rounds too much, so the dough is airy enough to form a hollow pocket.

5. Place the disks on the hot stone or baking sheet in the oven and bake for 3 to 5 minutes, or until they are puffed and light brown on top. Remove the pitas from the oven and wrap them in a kitchen towel for 5 minutes before serving.

A. Combine flour, yeast, salt, sugar, warm water, and olive oil in a food processor. Pulse until a ball forms.

B. Gradually stream in more warm water and process for an additional minute.

C. Cover the dough with a kitchen towel and let rise at room temperature for 30 to 45 minutes.

D. Refrigerate the risen dough for at least 15 minutes or up to 3 hours. Transfer to a lightly floured board.

E. Pat the dough into a log shape, then cut into 4 equal-sized pieces.

F. Gently tuck the edges of each dough piece beneath to form a round. Smooth the tops.

G. Transfer the whole board to the refrigerator for at least 10 minutes or up to 2 hours.

H. With the palm of your hand or a rolling pin, gently flatten each round into a 4- to 6-inch disk.

1. Place the disks on a hot pizza stone or baking sheet in the oven and bake for 3 to 5 minutes, or until puffy and browned on top.

J. Freshly baked pitas are ready for anything: stuffing, scooping, or wiping some hummus.

IN THE HAND

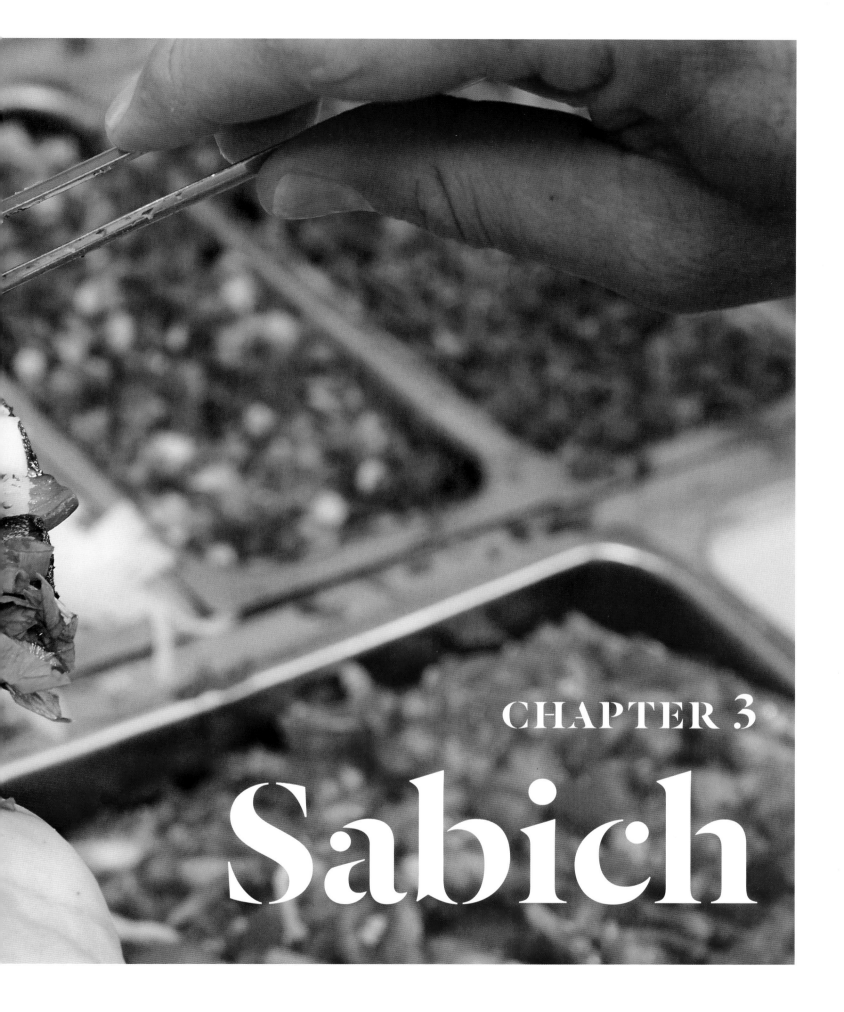

CHAPTER 3

Sabich

"Do you know how it feels to hold that warm overfilled sandwich in your hand? It feels like a beating heart."

If you think of sabich (pronounced saa-BEEK) as the story of Israel stuffed into a pita, you wouldn't be wrong. As anti-Semitic sentiment in the Arab world escalated around the time of Israeli Independence in 1948, Jews began streaming into the country from all over the Middle East, each community of immigrants bringing its own unique culinary traditions to the fledgling state.

For Iraqi Jews, this included the custom of eating fried or baked eggplant for breakfast on Shabbat morning, along with hard-boiled eggs and tehina. But these ingredients did not become sabich, or even Israeli, until they came together in a sandwich. And unlike other Israeli staples such as falafel, whose roots are Arabic, the story of sabich springs from the well of Jewish life.

In preparation for the Sabbath, observant Jews must finish cooking by sundown on Friday. For Iraqi Jews, this often means assembling t'bit, a stew of meat, grains, and vegetables. Similar to cholent or chamin, the t'bit cooks overnight on a hot plate and becomes a warm and hearty Shabbat lunch. On Saturday morning, however, Iraqi Jews needed a quick breakfast before heading off to synagogue. Hence sabich: The eggplant could be cooked the

Sabich Tchernichovsky

TEL AVIV | Just off Allenby Street, not far from the Carmel Market, Sabich Tchernichovsky is a relative newcomer, but their sabich *(above* and *previous spread)* is among the best in the country. Besides the rare addition of sliced boiled potatoes, the eggplant is sliced superthin so that when it's fried, it adds extra richness to the sandwich. As if to protect the interests of its guests, a sign that hangs in the shop reads: "No sale of sabich without eggplant."

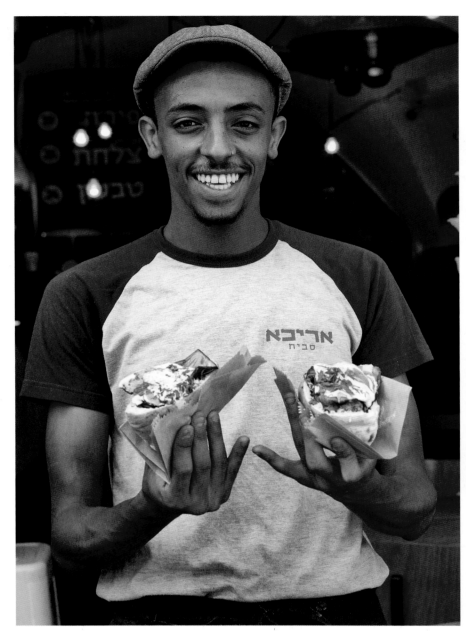

Aricha Sabich

JERUSALEM | Sabich is not native to Jerusalem, but Aricha, on Agrippas Street across from Machane Yehuda Market, is the best the city has to offer, according to Amit Aaronsohn, the Israeli food writer and television personality. Aricha salts its eggplant for three hours before rinsing it in hot water and letting it dry. Finally, it is fried to order, which makes all the difference.

day before and eaten at room temperature; the eggs could be plucked warm from the t'bit, where they had been slow-cooked in their shells to a creamy texture; and tehina and amba, the pickled mango sauce, were always on hand.

Sabich might have remained a culinary footnote if not for the influx of Iraqi Jews to Ramat Gan, a suburb of Tel Aviv, in the early 1950s. Inspired by the successful Israeli paradigm of "put it in a pita," enterprising immigrants saw the makings of a new sandwich. By the 1960s, open-air stalls selling sabich were commonplace in and around Tel Aviv, its ancestral homeland. Since then, sabich has steadily gained in popularity amid lively arguments about where to get the best—a sure sign of its Israeli status.

One of the best examples we found was at **Sabich Tchernichovsky**, named for the Tel Aviv street where it stands. Their version packs thinly sliced potatoes alongside the eggplant. Some argue that this addition comes straight from the Iraqi tradition: warm cooked potatoes were traditionally in t'bit. Others credit pure Israeli fusion, reflecting the Moroccan and Tunisian custom of eating cold potatoes in sandwiches.

The sabich at Tel Aviv's **HaKosem** is similarly enlightening. The owner, Arik Rosenthal, dredges thick slabs of eggplant in cornstarch before frying to give them an extra dimension of crunch, an inspiration he took from the Israeli obsession with putting French fries in such sandwiches as shawarma. "But fries stay crispy only for a minute," he says. "And then you ask yourself, 'Why did I eat all that?'" Not so his eggplant. We've boldly borrowed his technique.

What's in a Name?

There are at least three theories about how sabich got its name. If it seems strange that this is not settled fact for a sandwich that is already seventy years old, consider that food always tastes better eaten alongside a story.

The most straightforward explanation is that the name derives from the Arabic *sabach*, which means "breakfast." And it's true that the sandwich is based on the traditional Shabbat breakfast of Iraqi Jews. But if you ask for sabich in Iraq, you'll get blank stares. Nor does anything explain the transformation from *sabach* to *sabich*.

The second theory is that sabich is named for the person who first commercialized it. Most experts agree that in 1958 (or maybe 1961), Tzvi Halabi and his partner opened the first sabich kiosk on Uziel Street in Ramat Gan, the Tel Aviv suburb where Iraqi Jewish immigrants settled in droves. *Tzvi* is the Hebrew word for "deer"; in Arabic, it is *zabi*. And so the theory goes that, needing a name for his sandwich, Halabi simply named it after himself.

The last theory is enthusiastically (and maybe exclusively) put forward by Oved Daniel, the man who has done more than anyone to install sabich in the pantheon of great Israeli sandwiches. Since 1985, he has been serving excellent sabich, along with a healthy dose of shtick, from his centrally located stand, **Oved Sabich**, in Givatayim, just east of Tel Aviv.

According to Oved, the name *sabich* is an acronym for the main ingredients in the sandwich: *salat* (salad); *beitza* (egg); and *yoter chatzil* (more eggplant). This sounds a little like bullshit, and one wonders if Oved believes it himself. It's hard to tell. Straight-faced, he looks like an operative from the Israeli political thriller TV series *Fauda*, as hard-boiled as one of his eggs. But he can be playful, too. Watching Oved engage customers as he builds their pitas, you get why this is arguably the most popular sabich in all of Israel.

Newcomers are asked the score of an imaginary soccer game between HaPoel and Maccabi, two Tel Aviv soccer teams. HaPoel, whose uniforms are red, represents the fiery harif (hot sauce). Maccabi's yellow uniforms stand for amba (pickled mango sauce). A score of 2–1 in favor of HaPoel means you want two spoonfuls of harif and one spoonful of amba on your sandwich. Americans may instead be asked for the Los Angeles Lakers–Chicago Bulls score. No matter what it's called, in Oved's hands, it's a great meal.

In Jerusalem you're never far from an awesome religious experience. Here beliefs converge at the venerated Temple Mount, from the golden Dome of the Rock to the sacred Western Wall *(foreground)*.

CLASSIC MANGO AMBA
(page 79)

QUICK TEHINA SAUCE
(page 145)

PITA BREAD
(page 57)

HARISSA
(page 150)

CABBAGE

PARSLEY

TOMATOES

CUCUMBERS

HAMINADOS
(slow-roasted
eggs,
page 77)

HaKOSEM-STYLE
FRIED EGGPLANT
(page 74)

A. Stuff crispy fried eggplant into both sides of a wide-open pita.

B. Then add slices of the slow-roasted eggs called haminados.

C. Next, spoon in the freshest salad of diced cucumber and bright tomatoes.

D. Drizzle in the spicy sauces that make all the difference: amba, harissa, and tehina.

E. It takes both of Steve's hands to hold the sabich sandwich he's made. Doesn't get better than this.

Sabich: It's All About the Eggplant

Arik Rosenthal's cornstarch-dredged fried eggplant at **HaKosem**
(page 67) was a revelation to us. If there's a credible knock against
sabich, it's a reliance on the soft textures of pita, egg, and eggplant.
Adding a crunchy coating to the eggplant elegantly rebuts this critique.

HaKosem-Style Fried Eggplant

Serves 4

1 large eggplant
4 tablespoons kosher salt
½ cup cornstarch
Canola oil, for frying

1. Stripe the eggplant lengthwise with a vegetable peeler and trim off the ends. Slice into 12 roughly ½-inch-thick rounds. Sprinkle each of the eggplant slices on both sides with the salt and drain on a wire rack set on a baking sheet for 1 hour.

2. Pat the slices dry with paper towels. Put the cornstarch in a shallow bowl.

Dredge the eggplant in the cornstarch on both sides and tap off the excess.

3. Place a large skillet over medium heat and coat the bottom with oil. When the oil is hot, fry the eggplant in batches for about 2 minutes per side, or until golden. With a spatula, transfer the eggplant to paper towels to drain. Cool slightly before assembly.

Baked Eggplant
Serves 4

1   **large eggplant**
1   **tablespoon kosher salt**
2   **tablespoons canola oil**

Preheat the oven to 350°F. Stripe the eggplant lengthwise with a vegetable peeler and trim off the ends. Slice into 12 roughly ½-inch-thick rounds. Toss with the salt and oil in a large bowl. Place the eggplant in a single layer on a baking sheet and bake for 20 minutes, or until tender. Turn the slices and bake for a couple of minutes more to brown the other side. Let cool slightly before assembling.

Fire-Roasted Eggplant
Serves 4

Follow the process for Baked Eggplant but grill over medium heat for 3 to 4 minutes per side, or until charred and cooked through. Let cool slightly before assembling.

Haminados

Makes 6

6 large eggs
2 black tea bags
2 tablespoons Turkish coffee
Peels from 4 onions
2 quarts water

The prohibition against cooking on the Sabbath is responsible for a number of traditional Jewish stews that cook unattended overnight and are ready in time for Saturday lunch. Ashkenazi Jews have their cholent, and Iraqi Jews their t'bit. For Sephardic Jews, it's *hamin*, taken from the Latin word for "oven." *Haminados* (short for *huevos haminados*) refers to eggs that are slow-cooked in their shells in the hamin. In this recipe, tea and coffee replace the traditional meaty braising liquid. This slow cooking achieves a creamy texture unlike any we've experienced with traditional egg-cooking methods.

1. Preheat the oven to 200°F. Mix all the ingredients with the water in a large ovenproof pot. Cover and bake for at least 8 hours or up to 12 hours.

2. Remove the pot from the oven. Crack but do not peel the eggs, then return them to the pot with the liquid. Set the pot on the stovetop and cook over high heat, uncovered, until almost all the liquid has evaporated, about 20 minutes (watch closely; the eggs will explode if the pot gets too dry!). Cool the eggs on a plate, then peel and slice.

The Amba Mystique

The soul of sabich may be the marriage of the rich and bitter eggplant with the creamy, sweet egg, but it is amba, Iraqi pickled mango sauce, that brings balance to the relationship. Amba is powerfully redolent stuff—but sabich without amba is not sabich.

Amba is an adaptation of Indian mango pickle first brought back to Iraq by Jewish traders and quickly adopted as a pantry staple by Muslims, Christians, and Jews alike. Unlike its Indian cousin, amba uses ripe mangoes, balancing the sweet fruit with the pungency of fenugreek, mustard, and garlic and the earthiness of cumin, paprika, and turmeric. A touch of chile heat and the sour funk of fermentation makes a deep, exotic flavor profile. For Iraqi Jews, amba is the through line that connects their new home in Israel with their legacy as merchants and traders on the Indian subcontinent.

Arab Jews first came to India in the wake of the great Portuguese, Dutch, and British trading companies. They initially settled in Surat, on the Arabian Sea, before spreading to Mumbai and Kolkata (the British Colonial base in India), and deeper into Southeast Asia and China. These so-called Baghdadi Jews comprised a majority of Jews in Asia well into the twentieth century. In his memoir *Baghdad, Yesterday: The Making of an Arab Jew*, the Israeli writer Sasson Somekh recalls amba's pungent odor as one of the defining sensory memories of his Iraqi childhood. His mother would admonish him against the "contaminated" amba sold by street vendors: They had a perfectly good barrel of the genuine article at home.

According to Somekh, as soon as Iraqi Jews arrived in Israel in the late 1940s, they set up small amba factories. And in the true melting pot spirit of Israel, amba quickly made the jump from Iraqi sabich stands to the condiment bars of falafel and shawarma shops. But even we don't make amba from scratch if we need just a spoonful or two in a sauce or dressing. Amba in jars is perfect for that.

Classic Mango Amba

Makes about 1 cup

- 2 ripe mangoes, peeled, pitted, and chopped
- 1 small onion, finely chopped
- 1 large garlic clove, thinly sliced
- 1 teaspoon kosher salt
- 2 teaspoons mustard seeds
- 1½ teaspoons ground turmeric
- 1 teaspoon ground cumin
- 1 teaspoon crushed Aleppo pepper
- 1 teaspoon ground fenugreek
- 1 teaspoon smoked paprika

Kosher salt

Lemon juice

We sell golden jars of Galil amba, imported from Israel, at Goldie in Philadelphia, and other good prepared amba sauces are available online. But here's how to make your own.

1. Combine all the ingredients except the salt and lemon juice in a medium saucepan and cook over medium heat, stirring frequently, until the mangoes have broken down and the mixture has reduced by half, about 20 minutes.

2. Let the amba cool, then taste and add salt and a squeeze of lemon juice. Refrigerate in a covered container for up to 2 weeks.

MUSTARD SEEDS

CRUSHED ALEPPO
PEPPER

ONION

STRAWBERRIES

OLIVE OIL

GROUND CUMIN

GARLIC

LEMON

GROUND TURMERIC

MANGO

APPLE

KOSHER SALT

FENUGREEK

SMOKED PAPRIKA

Amba Variations

Over the years, we've learned that mango is not the only fruit that can be amba-tized. Applying the same methodology and spicing to apples, for example, yields Apple Amba, a terrific accompaniment to our potato-leek riff on sabich *(page 83)*. Strawberry Amba pairs perfectly with fried haloumi cheese and is a great accompaniment to spicy grilled merguez sausage. Amba's journey continues.

Apple Amba

Makes about 2 cups

- 2 tablespoons canola oil
- 4 medium apples, peeled, cored, and chopped
- 1 small onion, finely chopped
- 1 large garlic clove, thinly sliced
- 1 teaspoon kosher salt
- 2 teaspoons mustard seeds
- 1½ teaspoons ground turmeric
- 1 teaspoon ground cumin
- 1 teaspoon crushed Aleppo pepper
- 1 teaspoon ground fenugreek
- 1 teaspoon smoked paprika
- Kosher salt
- Lemon juice

Heat the oil in a medium saucepan. Add all the ingredients except the salt and lemon juice and cook over medium heat, stirring frequently, until the apples have broken down almost completely and the mixture has reduced by half, 20 to 25 minutes. Let the amba cool, then taste and add salt and a squeeze of lemon juice, as needed. Refrigerate in a covered container for up to 2 weeks.

Strawberry Amba

Makes about 1 cup

Follow the process for Apple Amba, substituting 1 quart strawberries, hulled and halved, for the apples.

Sabich HaSharon

HOD HaSHARON | We loved just stumbling upon this excellent version of sabich at this roadside kiosk, where a sign outside reads: "Without all the BS . . . the only original." Of course this isn't true, but it doesn't stand in the way of a great sandwich, either.

Oved Sabich

GIVATAYIM | Oved Daniel is the biggest name in sabich. He's devoted the last twenty-five-plus years to raising the profile of the sandwich from his small storefront window.

Just east of Tel Aviv, Givatayim is hardly a tourist destination, but visitors flock there to taste the most famous sabich in the world and to experience Oved's shtick in equal measure. They send him photos from everywhere, which he plasters on the inside wall of his shop. Oved's sabich is the standard-bearer, so it's difficult to say what sets his sandwiches apart besides nearly three decades of practice in making them.

I Can't Believe It's Not Eggplant!

It may seem antithetical to make sabich without eggplant. But the triumvirate of hard-boiled egg, amba, and a hearty vegetable is too appealing to cling to such orthodoxy. The crunch of a potato-leek latke, together with a creamy egg and spoonful of apple amba, makes a delicious variation for the fall and winter. We think it's especially good at home during Hanukkah. Similarly, maitake mushrooms, dredged in cornstarch and pan-fried until their edges turn crispy, become a vegetarian paradise when paired with strawberry amba. You won't even miss the eggplant!

Battered Maitake Mushrooms

Serves 4

- 2 large maitake (aka hen of the woods) mushrooms
- 1½ teaspoons kosher salt
- ½ cup cornstarch
- ¼ cup canola oil

Square off the edges of the mushroom clusters, then slice the mushrooms into ½- to ¾-inch-thick "steaks." Sprinkle with the salt. Put the cornstarch in a shallow bowl. Dredge the mushrooms in the cornstarch on both sides and tap off the excess. Heat the oil in a medium skillet over medium heat. Fry the mushrooms for 3 minutes per side, or until golden and crispy. Let cool slightly before serving.

Potato-Leek Latke

Makes 1 large latke (enough for 4 pitas)

- 2 medium russet or Yukon Gold potatoes, peeled and grated
- 3 leeks, whites only, thinly sliced and rinsed
- ¼ cup all-purpose flour
- 1½ teaspoons kosher salt
  Canola oil, for frying

1. Mix together the potatoes, leeks, flour, and salt in a large bowl. Set aside for 10 minutes to allow the potatoes to release some starch, which will help hold the latke together.

2. Pour about ¼ inch of canola oil into a medium skillet and place over medium-low heat. Make one big pancake by spooning the batter into the skillet and pressing it down evenly in the pan. Fry for 10 to 15 minutes per side, or until cooked through and crispy on the outside. Let cool slightly, then cut into wedges.

IN THE HAND

CHAPTER 4

Shawarma

"A great shawarma turning is one where you can see the layers, see how fresh it is."

—AVIHAI TSABARI, CERTIFIED GUIDE

The beauty of shawarma (and any spit-roasted meat) is that it bastes itself in its own fat and juices as it slowly turns in front of the fire. At a busy shawarma place, the meat on each sandwich hits the sweet spot between juicy and caramelized just as it spins into the carver's path and meets its destiny with the deft flick of a sharp knife. But with each untouched revolution of the spit, this ideal slips further away.

We sometimes wonder whether there actually is such a thing as great shawarma. There must be, because the name alone makes our mouths water.

The idea of crispy spit-roasted meat, shaved thin and rolled up inside a fresh-baked laffa bread with layered tehina, bright salad, tangy pickles, and piquant harif (Yemenite hot sauce), could entice us to trade our restaurant empire for just one bite. Though shawarma is everywhere in Israel, really good shawarma is hard to find. Low-quality meat, purchased preformed on a spit and delivered by large food-service companies, seems to be the norm. It's even worse in the U.S., where an impaled loaf of overspiced, emulsified ground meat frequently masquerades as shawarma.

And then there is the issue of time. How *long* has that meat been turning, turning, turning in front of that heat? Who knows? Is shawarma like the

Previous spread: At Shamsa, in the old market in Akko, turkey is basted with lamb fat. *This page:* The shawarma art form at one of our faves, HaKosem, in Tel Aviv.

Philly cheesesteak, a meat sandwich whose fame has surpassed its deliciousness? Fortunately, great shawarmas (and cheesesteaks) are still out there. The **Haj Kahil** family has lived in Jaffa for more than a century and has been in the restaurant business since 1973. Their corner restaurant near the Jaffa Clock Tower buzzes with activity late on a Friday night. Haj Kahil easily goes through four giant spits of meat in a single night, guaranteeing the customer perfectly cooked and perfumed meat, rolled in laffa fresh from the restaurant's own wood-fired taboon.

At **HaKosem**, which means "The Magician," in Tel Aviv, Arik Rosenthal uses only female turkey legs for his shawarma—he believes they're more tender than the male—layered with ground lamb fat. Countermen in white paper hats serve this superlative sandwich to some 1,500 customers a day. They could sell more, but they're working as fast as the spit can turn.

HaKosem

TEL AVIV | "Don't eat shawarma just anywhere in Israel!" counsels HaKosem's Arik Rosenthal. "You must look for a busy place." He should know. The Tel Aviv–born Arik (via Egypt and Romania) was a waiter in a coffee shop when the cook didn't show up. He opened HaKosem at twenty-six.

His meticulous approach to street food—HaKosem makes hummus nine times a day—might seem like overkill. But just look at his shawarma! Arik is like the best practitioners in Israel, those who've been doing it the same way, every day, for decades. "We don't really sell food," he says. "We sell three minutes of happiness."

Lamb Shoulder Shawarma

Serves 8

2½ tablespoons Shawarma Spice Blend #1 for Red Meat *(page 150)*

1 tablespoon kosher salt

1 (4-pound) boneless lamb shoulder, butterflied

2 tablespoons canola oil

Most of us don't have vertical roasting spits in the backyard, but we can still apply the principles of good shawarma at home. Forget about the theatricality of a revolving tower of meat: What matters is the right cut with a good amount of fat to prevent it from drying out as it cooks. A butterflied lamb shoulder, cured with spices, then rolled and tied, is a perfect example. Gentle roasting tenderizes the meat while it luxuriates in its own rendering fat—just like real shawarma!

When it cools down, thin slices are quickly seared in a hot cast-iron pan. Instead of the wrap, serve thick slices of that lamb alongside Rice Pilaf with Peas and Pistachios *(page 103)* and Caramelized Fennel *(page 103)* as the hero of your next dinner party. Or roll it all up in your own Druze Mountain Bread *(page 116)*.

1. Mix the Spice Blend and salt in a small bowl. Rub this mixture all over the lamb, cover, and refrigerate overnight.

2. The next day, preheat the oven to 450°F.

3. Roll up the lamb and tie it with butcher's twine. Put the lamb on a baking sheet or roasting pan and roast for 30 minutes, then reduce the heat to 275°F and roast for another 2½ to 3 hours, rotating every 30 minutes, or until a meat thermometer inserted into the center of the lamb registers 160°F. Remove from the oven and let cool to room temperature.

4. Wrap the lamb tightly in plastic and refrigerate for at least 3 hours or, preferably, overnight to make the lamb easier to slice.

5. To serve the shawarma, unwrap the lamb and slice it against the grain as thinly as you can. Place a cast-iron skillet over medium-high heat and add the oil. Fry the sliced lamb for about 3 minutes, or until it's hot and slightly crispy.

PICKLES

EVERYDAY SCHUG
(page 151)

CABBAGE

CUCUMBERS

HARISSA
(page 150)

QUICK TEHINA SAUCE
(page 145)

PARSLEY

TOMATOES

DRUZE MOUNTAIN BREAD
(page 116)

LAMB SHOULDER SHAWARMA
(page 91)

CHICKEN THIGH SHAWARMA
(page 100)

A. Thinly slice the roasted lamb shoulder *(page 91)* and brown it in a pan.

B. Use Druze Mountain Bread *(page 116)* or thin flatbread-like lavash for the wrap.

C. Spoon Quick Tehina Sauce *(page 145)* generously onto the middle of the wrap.

D. Spoon on the browned roast lamb, tomatoes, cukes, cabbage, pickles, and parsley.

E. Add the spice: harissa in drips, schug, and more tehina sauce.

F. Roll up the bread and "burrito" the ends to keep the insides tightly packed.

G. Wrapped shawarma in cross section: a thing of beauty and a joy forever. Until it's eaten!

When the Jaffa Clock
Tower comes into view,
you know good food is
sure to follow.

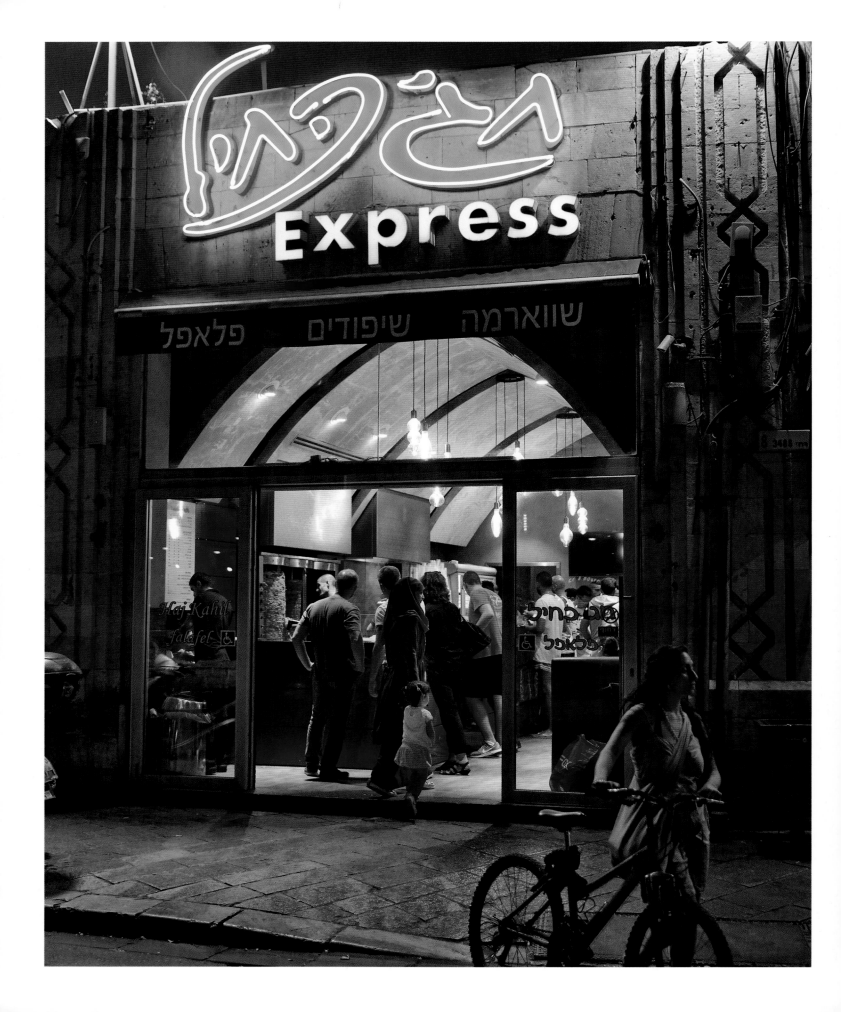

Haj Kahil

JAFFA | The Haj Kahil family has lived in Jaffa for over 120 years. Under Ottoman rule, they ferried dignitaries in horse-drawn carriages. For the last forty years, they've run restaurants, with commendable places located around the Jaffa Clock Tower.

At Haj Kahil Express, twin towers of rotating meat—turkey and lamb shawarma—animate the bright open kitchen. The later it gets, the more crowded it is, pulsing with the young beat of Jaffa's nightlife. Using a power tool resembling a circular saw, the cooks work quickly to shave meat from the spit and expertly roll it in laffa bread with vegetables and condiments. It's eaten as quickly as it's made.

A. Rub the chicken thighs with spices, then roll tightly in plastic wrap.

B. Refrigerate for at least two hours or up to 2 days. They'll be poached and refrigerated again before slicing.

Chicken Thigh Shawarma

Serves 6

1½ tablespoons Shawarma Spice Blend #2 for Poultry *(page 150)*

1½ teaspoons kosher salt

2 pounds skinless, boneless chicken thighs

2 tablespoons canola oil

In Israel, succulent and tender turkey shawarma layered with lamb fat gives the lamb version a run for its money. At home, chicken thighs can give the same juicy effect. We poach boneless thighs, then roll them in plastic wrap and chill them to firm them up, all the better to slice thin, uniform pieces to crisp in a pan. Our Shawarma Spice Blends *(page 150)* can be used interchangeably. Here we use a Yemenite-inspired blend, redolent of curry and turned golden by the turmeric.

1. Mix the Spice Blend with the salt in a small bowl. Rub the chicken thighs all over with the mixture and roll up. Place each seasoned and rolled thigh on a piece of plastic wrap and tightly roll each in the plastic, securing the wrap under the rolls. Refrigerate for at least 2 hours or up to 2 days.

2. Bring a medium pot of water to a simmer. Carefully lower the wrapped chicken rolls into the hot water and poach them for 15 minutes. Transfer to an ice bath, then drain and refrigerate for at least 2 hours or up to overnight.

3. When you're ready to serve the shawarma, unwrap the chicken and slice each roll thinly. Place a cast-iron skillet over medium-high heat and add the oil. Cook the sliced chicken, turning occasionally, for about 3 minutes, or until the pieces are slightly charred.

C. Sear the chicken slices in a hot skillet so they're slightly charred and very tasty.

D. Like the lamb, layer the chicken on the bread wrap, then heap with vegetables and sauces.

E. Then slice the uniquely flavorful chicken shawarma to reveal its juicy contents.

Rice Pilaf with Peas and Pistachios

Serves 8

This savory rice is just the thing to sop up the richly flavored juices from the Shawarma Spice–rubbed roast lamb shoulder *(page 91)*.

¼ cup olive oil

1 onion, minced

3 garlic cloves, thinly sliced

2 teaspoons kosher salt

½ teaspoon ground turmeric

½ teaspoon ground coriander

½ teaspoon ground cumin

½ cup pistachios, ground in a spice grinder

2 cups white basmati rice

4 cups water

2 cups fresh or frozen English peas

½ cup chopped fresh parsley

1. Preheat the oven to 350°F. Heat the oil in an ovenproof pot over medium heat. Add the onion, garlic, and salt and cook for about 5 minutes, or until the onion is translucent but not browned. Add all the spices, the pistachios, and the rice and sauté for another minute, or until fragrant. Stir in the water and cover the pot. Bake for 45 minutes, or until the rice is cooked through. Keeping the pot covered, let it stand off the heat to steam for about 10 minutes.

2. Meanwhile, blanch the peas in boiling water for 2 minutes, then shock them in an ice-water bath to lock in the color. Just before serving, stir the peas and parsley into the pilaf.

Caramelized Fennel

Makes about 3 cups

2 tablespoons canola oil

4 fennel bulbs, julienned

2 teaspoons kosher salt

Heat the oil in a medium cast-iron skillet over medium-low heat. Add the fennel and salt and cook for 45 minutes, stirring frequently to prevent burning, or until golden brown and crispy.

Turkey Paillard

Serves 6

1 (2- to 2½-pound) skinless, boneless turkey breast

¼ cup olive oil

1 tablespoon kosher salt

2 teaspoons za'atar

1 teaspoon ground coriander

4 garlic cloves, minced

½ cup fresh cilantro, chopped

Applying a shawarma-inspired spice blend to lean grilled turkey breast elevates this mild meat above its workaday existence as a lunchtime staple. Served over Opera-Style Chopped Salad, inspired by our favorite Yemenite restaurant in Hadera, it's a light and flavorful meal.

1. Butterfly the turkey and pound it evenly to a ½-inch thickness, then slice thickly.

2. Mix the oil, salt, za'atar, coriander, garlic, and cilantro in a shallow bowl. Add the turkey and coat it in the seasonings. Cover and refrigerate for at least 2 hours or up to 24 hours.

3. When you're ready to cook the turkey, place a cast-iron skillet over medium-high heat. Sear the turkey pieces for 5 minutes per side, or until cooked through. Let the turkey rest, then slice thickly on the bias.

Opera-Style Chopped Salad

Serves 6

4 cucumbers, peeled and chopped

2 plum tomatoes, chopped

1 red bell pepper, seeded and chopped

1 cup chopped Napa cabbage

1 red onion, minced

1 tablespoon olive oil

Juice of 2 lemons

1 tablespoon kosher salt

1 cup chopped fresh dill

Mix all of the ingredients in a bowl. Taste and add more salt as needed.

Sometimes vegetables are set below the shawarma to catch the succulent drippings as the meat turns.

Bandora Shawarma

JERUSALEM | Bandora, an Israeli mini chain, has turned the world of shawarma on its side—literally. Unlike virtually all other shawarma we have ever seen, Bandora spit-roasts its version horizontally over a bed of live charcoal. As with kebabs, this method perfumes the meat with the smoke created when the dripping fat hits the charcoal below.

Cauliflower Shawarma

Serves 6

2 quarts water

2 cups kosher salt

2 tablespoons Shawarma Spice Blend #3 for Vegetables *(page 150)*

1 (1½- to 2-pound) head cauliflower, leaves removed

4 tablespoons canola oil

For a dramatic vegetable "shawarma" option, we rub a whole head of cauliflower with a sweet and savory spice blend headlined by baharat, then oven-roast it. But first we soak the cauliflower in a spiced brine to season the interior. Served whole with Quick Tehina Sauce *(page 145)* on the side, this bronzed brassica makes an impressive centerpiece. You can also cool it down, then sear the florets in a cast-iron pan to make a vegan shawarma sandwich, piling the seared florets into a waiting pita with all the shawarma fixings.

1. Mix together the water, salt, and 1 tablespoon of the Shawarma Spice Blend in a large pot. Warm over medium heat, whisking constantly, until the salt is fully dissolved. Let the mixture cool completely. Brine the cauliflower in the spiced water for 2 hours at room temperature.

2. Preheat the oven to 450°F. When the brining time is almost up, add 2 tablespoons of the canola oil to the remaining Spice Blend in a small bowl and stir well to form a paste. Remove the cauliflower from the brine, shake it off, then rub most of the spice paste over it, saving a spoonful for searing, if you like. Transfer the cauliflower to a rimmed

baking sheet and roast for 45 minutes, or until browned and tender.

3. Remove the cauliflower from the oven, let it cool a little, then carve and serve like the juicy roast it is. Or cut the cauliflower into bite-size florets, transfer to a large bowl, and add the remaining canola oil and the reserved spice paste. Toss well. Sear the florets in a very hot cast-iron pan for 3 to 4 minutes, or until nicely charred.

HaShomer

CARMEL MARKET | Literally translated as "the Guard," this boisterous fourteen-seat counter and satellite dining room offers thoughtful remixes of Israeli classics, like Iraqi kebabs on challah or a Tel Aviv version of Jerusalem mixed grill stuffed into a European roll. The spiced and roasted whole cauliflower makes a deeply satisfying meatless meal.

CHAPTER 5
Druze Moun

tain Bread

> *"In the ancient world, the term* flatbread *would have been redundant. All bread was flat. The earth was flat, too."*

The Druze are an ethno-religious group that split from Islam during the early eleventh century. Today the population is concentrated in Syria, Lebanon, and Israel. During the War of Independence, many Druze fought on behalf of Israel, earning their community both official recognition in the new Jewish state and a reputation for patriotism and loyalty that continues to this day.

Most of the approximately 150,000 Israeli Druze live in the verdant hills of the Galilee, where the olive oil is green and the za'atar is greener. Roadside stands dot the region, and you can often find Druze women cooking mountain bread to feed hungry travelers. Eating it in the sunshine, overlooking an olive grove or a field of wildflowers, you can sometimes catch a glimpse of the Sea of Galilee.

The Druze cook their bread on a convex steel griddle, or sajj, which typically sits over a gas or propane burner, perfect for mobile installations. The convex shape of the griddle prevents the dough from shrinking as it cooks. (We find it handy to use an upside-down steel wok—or large skillet—at home; *see page 116*).

Previous spread: Our homemade flatbread is layered with labneh and fresh herbs. *This page:* At Tel Aviv's Carmel Market, a Druze woman shows how it's done.

Druze mountain bread slathered with chocolate spread is a favorite childhood treat in Israel. But we think the best way to eat it is the most traditional: spread thickly with labneh, generously sprinkled with za'atar and olive oil, and folded into a triangle. And you don't have to drive all the way to the Galilee to eat it. A stall in the Carmel Market in Tel Aviv offers this simple delicacy, cooked by Druze women in traditional dress. Or better yet, you can easily make it at home.

Not only is this one of the most uncomplicated breads we've ever made, it's also among the most rewarding. The dough has a bit of yeast in it, but it is not nearly as temperamental as pita dough, making it the perfect wrap for a sandwich or a snack on its own.

A World of Flatbread

The earliest breads were thin pancake-like loaves baked on rocks—and later terra-cotta griddles—heated over a fire.

With the oven came slightly thicker loaves that could fully bake before burning. Much later, Levantine bakers developed a method of baking lean, wet, yeast-raised rounds in a very hot oven to reliably produce a pocket. This is pita (*khubz* in Arabic), what Israelis instinctively reach for when sandwiches are on the line.

But there is a whole world of flatbreads, each with its own unique characteristics and advantages. Laffa, the Iraqi version, is cooked in a traditional beehive-shaped oven

Druze mountain bread bubbles and chars on a convex steel griddle at Carmel Market.

called a taboon. On a recent visit to **Haj Kahil** restaurant in Jaffa, I found myself doing what I do most nights at home at Zahav: making laffa at the taboon (*far left* and *top left*). Laffa dough is similar to pita (but it does not form pita's trademark pocket). The dough is stretched into a large round over a cloth-covered cushion, then slapped with a flourish against the interior wall of the oven, where it cooks on one side only. The result is charred, crispy, soft, and chewy—all at the same time.

The word *laffa* translates to "wrap"—a reminder that the large flatbread is ideal for rolling around sandwich fillings. In many Israeli falafel and shawarma shops, you can choose laffa or pita. Laffa is great for shawarma, where the tight roll holds everything in balance and is less leak-prone than a stuffed pita.

Laffa has many analogues in the flatbread universe. Saluf is the Yemenite version—also taboon-baked and virtually indistinguishable from laffa, except for an added bit of ground fenugreek. Naan, too, is from the same flatbread family tree. We associate it with Indian cuisine, but it's actually the Farsi word for "bread." It's also the Afghan word for bread. And the Bukharan word. Whether baked in a tannur, tandoor, or taboon—all cylindrical ovens with the heat source on the bottom—these flatbreads are remarkably similar.

Good food ideas travel fast. The ancient Silk Road trade routes that connected the Mediterranean to the Far East helped spread bread recipes over vast sections of the planet. Lavash, the common term for unleavened (or lightly leavened) flatbread, is another well-traveled archetype that has made it to America. Much of the lavash we encounter here is dry and characterless—popular in soggy, premade sandwich wraps. But the real-deal lavash, whether baked in a taboon or more likely cooked on a griddle, is a staple on Armenian, Azerbaijani, and Georgian tables. In Lebanon it's often referred to as mountain bread; in Israel it's often referred to as Druze pita or Druze mountain bread.

Although laffa is the most common flatbread in Israel, we love making mountain bread because it's so simple and forgiving. A bit of yeast and oil in the dough help keep it soft for a long time, so you can cover a batch of baked flatbreads with a towel until you're ready to use them.

Druze Mountain Bread

Makes 8 to 10

3 cups bread flour

1 cup all-purpose flour

1 teaspoon instant yeast

1½ teaspoons kosher salt

3 tablespoons olive oil, plus more for coating the bowl

1½ cups warm water

Druze mountain bread works perfectly in the home kitchen because it's so simple. And it's the best use of your wedding-registry wok currently gathering dust in a cabinet. Simply invert the wok over a gas burner on medium-high heat, and in three minutes you have your own Druze oven. No wok? No worries. Just divide the dough into smaller pieces and make the breads in a large, hot skillet.

Rolled out on a floured board, then hand-stretched with your fists until you can read an Israeli newspaper through it, the dough has the quality of soft fabric. The result is not unlike a flour tortilla, but the yeast in the dough causes it to bubble and char, adding flavor and creating a lighter, less dense texture.

1. Combine the two flours, the yeast, salt, 3 tablespoons oil, and the water in the bowl of a stand mixer fitted with the dough hook. Mix for 4 to 5 minutes. The dough will be sticky. Rub a large bowl with olive oil. Scrape the dough out into the oiled bowl, cover with a kitchen towel, and let rise at room temperature for 45 minutes to 1 hour.

2. Once the dough has risen and doubled in volume, scrape it onto a floured board and pat into a long log shape. Cut it into 8 to 10 equal pieces. (If you're using a large skillet instead of a wok, portion the dough into 10 to 12 smaller pieces.) Cover with a kitchen towel and let rest for 30 minutes at room temperature.

3. Place a ball of dough on a floured board and flip to coat with flour. With your fingers, pat it out to a 6-inch round and roll it out until it's about double that size, using just enough flour to keep it from sticking. Pick up the dough and lay it over your fists. To stretch it, spread your fists apart, rotate the dough, and repeat until it's evenly thin and translucent in some spots. (You can also hold the dough on one end with both hands and let gravity do some of the work.) Don't worry if small holes appear.

4. Place a metal wok upside down over a gas burner set to medium-high heat. (For electric stoves, place a large cast-iron skillet or griddle over medium-high heat.) Let the wok heat up for at least 5 minutes. Have a damp kitchen towel handy for cleaning off the wok between breads.

5. Lay one piece of dough over the wok like a blanket and cook just until bubbling and browned on the bottom, no longer than 30 seconds. Remove with long-handled tongs and wipe off excess flour or dough from the wok with the towel. Repeat with the remaining dough. Set the cooked breads aside and cover with a kitchen towel.

A. After the dough has risen, cut it into pieces, rest it, and roll out into 6-inch circles on a floured board.

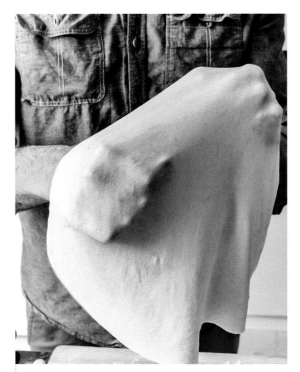

B. Now spread your fists beneath the dough and stretch and rotate until it doubles in size.

C. Heat a wok over a gas burner for 5 minutes, then lay a piece of stretched dough over the top.

D. Cook the dough until bubbling and browned on the bottom, no longer than 30 seconds.

E. Remove the bread with long tongs and transfer to a tray. Cover the cooked breads with a kitchen towel.

IN THE HAND

CHAPTER 6

Jerusalem

Grill

"This dish has become a metaphor for every Israeli household, which is a mixed grill of nationalities."

It's a Tuesday night in August in Jerusalem, and the brutal daytime heat has given way to the cooler temperatures that settle on the city at nightfall. The streets are full and the lively crowd at **Hatzot**, a grill restaurant on Agrippas Street just below the Machane Yehuda Market, joyfully overflows onto the sidewalk tables.

Hatzot literally means "midnight," perhaps the best time to consume the restaurant's signature dish. At that late hour and presumably a few beers deep, one may be more inclined toward eating a pita stuffed with chicken livers, spleens, hearts, and gizzards. But we are already inhaling this sandwich and it's only 9 o'clock. Dating just to the 1960s, Jerusalem's signature fast food is so fitting, it became the title of a hit Israeli TV show, *Meorav Yerushalmi*.

There is something deeply savory about this mix: The organ meats are turbocharged with the concentrated essence of chicken, heavily perfumed with grilled onions and a secret blend of spices. No salad embellishes this sandwich, just tehina and pickles. The improbable sweetness of the meat resonates with a deep, primal hunger.

Previous spread: Grill cooks in their element at Hatzot in Jerusalem. *This page:* It may be ancient, but this view of Jerusalem never gets old.

Hatzot

JERUSALEM | We've found that the appeal of the Jerusalem mixed grill sandwich increases as the night wears on. The lively crowds at Hatzot spill out of the restaurant onto tables on the sidewalk. The sandwich is washed down with icy lemonanna, *opposite*, made green with lots of mint.

Offal, the organs and entrails of a butchered animal, is a polarizing subject.

We're not surprised to learn that the origin of the Jerusalem mixed grill is clouded with competing claims and tenuous history. What is surprising is how a dish that's rarely seen outside of Jerusalem—and far from ubiquitous inside the city—can be so widely known and celebrated. The answer may lie in Jerusalem itself, a city not generally known for its food but one with a pretty good brand nonetheless. The dish may have been a stroke of marketing genius by a restaurant that decided to take "inner things" (the term sounds more poetic in Hebrew: *dvarim pnimi'im*) and cloak them in the aura of the world's most venerated city.

But which restaurant? The Ajami brothers, who claim to have originated Jerusalem mixed grill, opened Hatzot as a small counter in the shadow of the market in 1970, serving kebabs and grilled meats. At the end of the day, so the story goes, the brothers took all the leftover odds and ends, grilled them in lamb fat with onions and spices, and stuffed them into a pita. This tasty and inexpensive sandwich became an after-hours legend. In the nearly fifty years that have passed, the Ajami brothers have grown Hatzot into a large and lively restaurant, now occupying several storefronts on Agrippas. And they did it on the back of a sandwich made from things no one wanted.

The Ajamis' claim seems credible, except that at least one other nearby restaurant, also famous for its Jerusalem mixed grill, opened earlier, in 1969. What's not contested is the idea that Jerusalem mixed grill was "invented" near and, to a great extent, is a product of Machane Yehuda Market, aka "The Shuk." Literally translated as "Jewish market," Machane Yehuda dates to the late nineteenth century and was designed to serve the growing population living outside the walls of Jerusalem's Old City. With more than 250 vendors, it is the largest shuk in Israel. The crowds build from busy to insane throughout the week as Friday approaches and people scramble to prepare for Shabbat. Locals jostle with tourists in a daily struggle to get their shopping done, while merchants hawk produce, fish, meat, spices, and anything else you can imagine.

And everyone has to eat! Like any working market, the area in and around Machane Yehuda teems with restaurants catering to shoppers and workers, and their menus teem with what is available at the shuk. At the end of the day, the shuk's poultry butchers are left with a quantity of super-fresh chicken offal, and restaurants like Hatzot are more than happy to snap it up at a good price. For adventurous eaters in the know, these cuts provide a thrilling and cheap reward. And for the less adventurous, a few drinks before midnight can help improve their courage.

Jerusalem Mixed Grill

Serves 4

CARAMELIZED ONIONS

- 2 tablespoons olive oil
- 1 large onion, thinly sliced
- 1 teaspoon plus a pinch of kosher salt
- 6 skin-on, boneless chicken thighs, skin removed and reserved, meat chopped
- 1 cup chicken livers, cleaned and coarsely chopped
- 1 cup chicken hearts, cleaned and halved (optional)
- 2 teaspoons ground turmeric
- 1 teaspoon ground cumin
- 1 teaspoon ground fenugreek
- 1 teaspoon baharat
- 1 teaspoon ground cinnamon
- ½ lemon

Rice or Pita Bread (*page 57*), pickles, and Quick Tehina Sauce (*page 145*), **for serving**

Offal is a polarizing subject. Many people can't get past the idea of it, much less its flavor, which can range from mild to downright gamy depending on the animal, the organ, and its freshness. Chicken offal is relatively tame and provides a good introduction to the genre. There's even a word for it—giblets—that sounds much cuter than offal. Giblets are often included when you buy a whole chicken, which is a great way to ease into cooking offal. Utilizing every part of the chicken feels good, too, and responsible.

Our recipes call for a mix of chicken livers and hearts, anchored by chicken thighs. Although Jerusalem mixed grill traditionally depends on giblets, it's the spicing (as with shawarma) that gives the dish its authentic flavor. So if you favor chicken thighs (turkey works great, too), or you can't wrap your mind around hearts and livers, by all means, use only thigh meat.

1. MAKE THE CARAMELIZED ONIONS: Heat the oil in a medium saucepan over medium heat, then add the onion and a pinch of salt and cook, stirring, until soft and translucent, about 5 minutes. Reduce the heat to medium-low and cook, stirring every few minutes, until the onion is caramelized, 30 to 45 minutes. Lower the heat if the onion begins to burn; add a splash of water if it seems too dry. Set the caramelized onions aside.

2. Mince the skins of 2 chicken thighs, heat a cast-iron skillet to very hot, and crisp the skins, turning once. You can crisp the remaining skins and reserve to top a salad or hummus.

3. Toss the chicken livers, hearts, and thigh meat in a large bowl with the turmeric, cumin, fenugreek, baharat, cinnamon, and the remaining teaspoon salt. Add to the hot skillet and sear, without stirring, for a minute or two, then cook over medium-high heat for about 5 minutes more. Add a squeeze of lemon juice.

4. Remove from the heat, transfer the meat to a bowl, and stir in the caramelized onions. Serve the mixed grill in a bowl over rice, or stuff it into Pita Bread with pickles and Quick Tehina Sauce.

A. Toss the chicken livers, hearts, and thigh pieces with spices and sear in a hot cast-iron skillet.

B. Turn, sear, and add a squeeze of lemon juice to the hot skillet.

C. Stir the caramelized onions into the mixed grill and serve over rice or stuff in pita.

Jerusalem Grill Rice Pilaf with Pine Nuts

Serves 4

¼ cup olive oil

1 large onion, thinly sliced

1½ tablespoons plus a pinch of kosher salt

1 cup chicken hearts, cleaned and chopped

1 pound skinless, boneless chicken thighs, chopped

2 teaspoons ground turmeric

1 teaspoon ground cumin

1 teaspoon ground fenugreek

1 teaspoon baharat

1 teaspoon ground cinnamon

2 cups jasmine rice

1 cup chicken livers, cleaned and pureed in a food processor

4 cups hot water

Chopped fresh cilantro, for topping

½ cup pine nuts, toasted, for topping

Much loved in the American South as dirty rice, this is a soulful one-pot meal. The livers are pureed before cooking and dissolve into the rice, leaving behind their deeply savory shadow.

1. Heat the oil in a large saucepan over medium heat. When it's hot, add the onion and a pinch of salt and cook, stirring, until soft and translucent, about 5 minutes. Reduce the heat to medium-low and cook, stirring, until the onion is caramelized, 20 to 30 minutes. Lower the heat if the onion begins to burn; add a splash of water if it seems too dry. Set aside.

2. Meanwhile, preheat the oven to 350°F. Toss the chicken hearts and thigh pieces with the turmeric, cumin, fenugreek, baharat, and cinnamon in a large bowl. Heat a cast-iron skillet over medium-high heat. When the skillet is very hot, add the hearts and thighs and sear, without stirring, for a minute or two. Transfer to the saucepan, then add the rice. Cook for 1 minute over medium heat, stirring constantly, then stir in the pureed chicken livers.

3. Dissolve the remaining 1½ tablespoons salt in the hot water and pour over the rice mixture. Cover tightly and bake for 30 minutes, or until the rice is tender. Remove from the oven and top with the caramelized onions and a scattering of cilantro leaves and pine nuts.

Long past midnight and the scene is still lively at Jerusalem's Hatzot, near the Machane Yehuda Market.

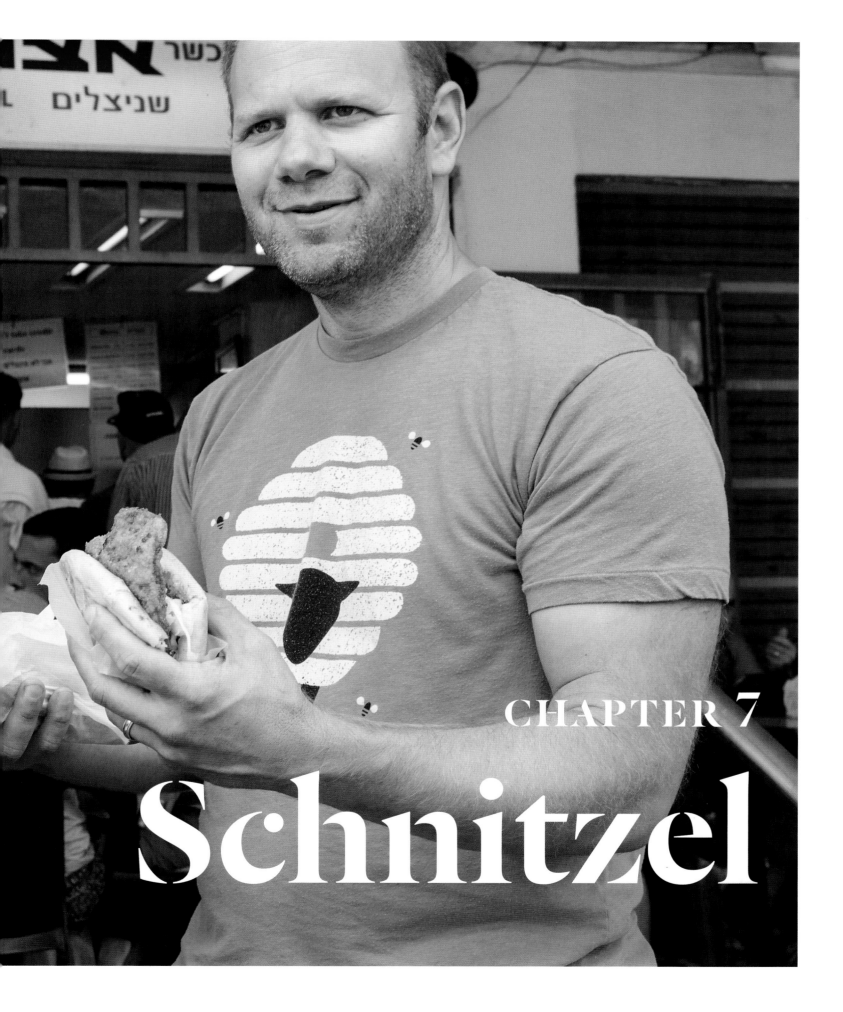

CHAPTER 7

Schnitzel

*"Does the schnitzel platter
come with rice?"
"No, just lots of schnitzel."*

—OVERHEARD AT ETZEL TZION, TEL AVIV

Schnitzel was one of the first foods that Jews brought to Palestine when they began arriving at the turn of the twentieth century, and over time it has become something of a national dish. Many of the original Jewish settlers were German; veal was their reference point, but because chicken and turkey were more affordable and available in Israel, they quickly became the schnitzel standard.

During the waves of immigration surrounding Israeli Independence (and in the decade of austerity that followed), women of all nationalities were taught this inexpensive meal made with accessible ingredients. As a new Israeli identity coalesced around the notion of a modern, independent Jewish state, Old World traditions were discarded in favor of food with a rugged informality. Israelis' affection for schnitzel was surpassed only by their dread of eating it so often. And so schnitzel was relegated to the bottom of the heap, where it eventually found work on army bases and in the cafeterias of major tourist attractions.

Schnitzel never really went away, but it was never really cool, either. This is hard to reconcile because we're essentially talking about fried chicken, which is one of the best things to ever happen to a bird. The crumb coating

protects the lean meat and keeps it juicy while adding the all-important crunch factor.

Some of the best schnitzel in Tel Aviv can be found at **Etzel Tzion**, a well-worn counter on the corner of HaYarkon and Trumpeldor Streets, just one block from the beach. Tzion opened in 1989 and gives off anything but an Old World vibe. Shirtless surfers in flip-flops shuffle forward in line, awaiting sustenance so they can conquer a few more waves. It is a busy stand, which helps assure that your sandwich is made with schnitzel so fresh that the oil on its surface is still sizzling when it's handed to you. Eaten with the usual suspects of chopped salad, pickles, tehina, and hot sauce, it makes a convincing argument that everything old is new again.

Though perhaps not as iconic as falafel or as sexy as shawarma, the schnitzel sandwich demonstrates that the surest way to rehabilitate something in Israel is simply to stuff it inside a pita.

Chicken Schnitzel

Serves 4

4 skinless, boneless chicken breasts

4 large eggs

2 tablespoons Hawaij Spice Blend *(page 150)*

2 cups matzo meal

2 teaspoons plus a pinch of kosher salt

¼ cup canola oil

Pita Bread *(page 57)* **with avocado and tomato slices, sprinkled with za'atar; or Yellow Rice** *(page 237)*, **Chopped Salad** *(page 187)*, **and Herbed Tehina,** *(page 45)* **for serving**

Traditional schnitzel breading procedure calls for dredging the meat in flour, followed by a dip in egg wash and a final coating in bread crumbs. A common problem with breaded food is that steam gets between the meat and the breading and drives them apart. If you've ever taken a bite of fried chicken and the entire crispy crust has just pulled right off, you know what I'm talking about. The express purpose of the flour in this process is supposedly to improve the adhesion of crust to meat. But I'm calling bullshit on this.

Recently I was flipping through a cookbook put together by bereaved parents of fallen Israeli soldiers, and I came across a recipe for schnitzel. Against all kitchen orthodoxy, the procedure had you soak the chicken in beaten whole eggs seasoned with hawaij, then coat it in bread crumbs and fry it. I was immediately intrigued. Was skipping the flour dredge a home cook's shortcut or a deliberate upending of standard breading procedure?

Of course we tried this method right away at Zahav, and it works so well it has become our standard schnitzel technique. The advantages are threefold: First, it saves the time and mess of the flouring step. Second, we can season the beaten eggs with salt and spices, essentially creating a brine for the chicken that makes it both juicier and tastier. And third, the crust (we use matzo meal here) sticks to the chicken better. It just goes to show you can't believe everything they teach you in culinary school.

1. Slice each chicken breast in half horizontally and pound (with a mallet or the back of a heavy pan) to an even ¼-inch thickness. In a shallow baking dish, beat the eggs with the hawaij. Place the chicken in the dish and turn to coat. Cover and refrigerate for 4 hours or up to overnight.

2. Place the matzo meal in a shallow dish and stir in the 2 teaspoons salt. Dredge the chicken in the matzo meal and set aside.

3. Heat the oil in a large cast-iron skillet over medium-high heat. Add the chicken, one or two pieces at a time, and cook until golden and crispy, about 3 minutes per side. Drain the chicken on paper towels, transfer to a plate, and sprinkle with a pinch of salt. Serve hot in pitas with avocado, tomato, and za'atar, or on a platter with Yellow Rice, Chopped Salad, and Herbed Tehina.

Zucchini Schnitzel

Serves 6

Fresh, thick slices of summer squash make unusual but no less delightful crispy schnitzel, topped with shipka hot peppers.

Substitute 2 large zucchini for the chicken breasts in Chicken Schnitzel *(page 134)*. Cut the zucchini in half lengthwise, then in half crosswise (but don't pound them!). Use the same egg-hawaij dip and the matzo meal coating. Follow the process for Chicken Schnitzel.

SHIPKA HOT PEPPERS are native to Bulgaria and, because they're bright orange, are sometimes called Bulgarian carrot peppers. Legend has it that the seeds were smuggled from behind the Iron Curtain in the 1980s. The pale green pickled shipka peppers are now ubiquitous on Israeli condiment bars. They pack about the same heat as jalapeños and are great with fried foods like falafel and, of course, schnitzel.

Etzel Tzion

TEL AVIV | Schnitzel doesn't get better than eating it stuffed in a pita after a day at the beach. And Etzel Tzion is a delightfully retro place to pick one up. The tiny storefront was here before schnitzel became cool again, and it will remain long after it returns to being old-fashioned.

CHAPTER 8
Hummus

"We believe 5-Minute Hummus to be a medium step forward for mankind."

When we wrote *Zahav*, we thought we knew everything there was to know about hummus. What more could we possibly have to say? Well, as it turns out, quite a lot. We've been elbows deep in hummus at Dizengoff, the little hummusiya we opened in Center City Philadelphia in 2014 (and later at Chelsea Market in New York). We've spent the last five years with hummus on the brain, and we have some thoughts.

Israelis make hummus at home infrequently, for the simple reason that they have easy access to excellent fresh hummus at their local hummusiyas. Even their supermarket hummus is a respectable stand-in. In Israel hummus basically comes out of the faucets.

That's not the case here in the U.S., at least until there is a Dizengoff in every town. Shelf-stable supermarket hummus can be very tasty, but it can also be stiff and sharp and generally not suited to be the centerpiece of a meal. It's also fairly expensive compared to homemade. And while making hummus from *dried* chickpeas is quite easy and extremely rewarding, it's not exactly an everyday project. Between the overnight soaking of the chickpeas and the hours of tending them as they cook, it takes planning and patience, things not always in ready supply when you're trying to get dinner on the table. Because hummus is everyday food—ridiculously satisfying, rich,

and healthy—we wanted to develop a recipe that you could make every day.

Enter 5-Minute Hummus. You will literally spend more time cleaning your food processor than putting this recipe together. It calls for two cans of chickpeas and a standard-size jar of tehina, so there's no measuring, extra bowls, or utensils to clean.

Canned chickpeas have a bad reputation in the hummus world. Canned beans are cooked to retain their shape and integrity, but when we cook chickpeas for hummus from scratch, we deliberately overcook them until they turn to mush. This is the secret to ultra-creamy hummus (that, and a $15,000 food processor). In recent times we have been conditioned to think of *canned* as a dirty word—the opposite of farm-to-table sanctimony. But you just have to open a can of succulent tomatoes in February to know that this is not a black-and-white issue. And when it comes to chickpeas, there's absolutely nothing wrong with the canned variety. True, canned chickpeas in a home food processor will never make hummus quite as smooth as what we make at Dizengoff. But it will taste every bit as delicious.

We know what you're thinking: Aren't you afraid someone is going to come along with four-minute hummus and beat you at your own game? No, we are not. We've tried four-minute hummus. And it is terrible.

Abu Hassan

JAFFA | Abu Hassan, *left* and *above,* is arguably the most famous hummusiya of them all. Of the two locations, you'll know you're at the busier one when you're (not so) politely encouraged to eat quickly. Go early for the Hummus Complet, with foul, tehina, and boiled chickpeas. Add a hit of chile-infused lemon juice and scoop up some hummus with a raw onion petal if you dare.

GROUND CUMIN   ICE WATER   KOSHER SALT

TEHINA   CHICKPEAS   GARLIC   LEMONS

5-Minute Hummus with Quick Tehina Sauce

Makes about 4 cups (4 servings)

QUICK TEHINA SAUCE

- 1 garlic clove
- Juice of 1 lemon
- 1 (16-ounce) jar tehina
- 1 tablespoon kosher salt
- 1 teaspoon ground cumin
- 1 to 1½ cups ice water

HUMMUS

- 2 (15-ounce) cans chickpeas, drained and rinsed

1. MAKE THE TEHINA SAUCE: Nick off a piece of the garlic (about a quarter of the clove) and drop it into a food processor.

2. Squeeze the lemon juice into the food processor. Pour the tehina on top, making sure to scrape it all out of the container, and add the salt and cumin.

3. Process until the mixture looks peanut-buttery, about 1 minute.

4. Stream in the ice water, a little at a time, with the motor running. Process just until the mixture is smooth and creamy and lightens to the color of dry sand. Now you have Quick Tehina Sauce!

5. MAKE THE HUMMUS: Add the chickpeas to the tehina sauce and process for about 3 minutes, scraping the sides of the bowl as you go, until the chickpeas are completely blended and the hummus is smooth and uniform in color.

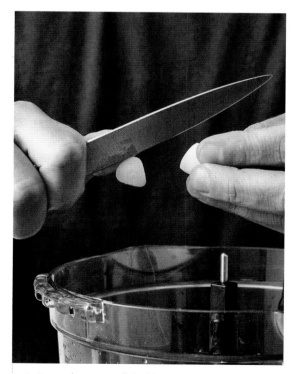

A. Forget the over-garlicked hummus—ours is perfumed by just a "nick" of one clove.

B. Squeeze fresh lemon juice right into the food processor with a handy citrus juicer.

C. Pour a whole 16-ounce container of tehina right into the food processor, scraping out the jar well.

D. Add cumin and salt to the mixture.

E. Process until it looks peanut-buttery, then, still mixing, add ice water a bit at a time.

F. Now you have Quick Tehina Sauce, which can be used in so many ways.

G. It's the chickpeas that make it hummus, and we happily use good canned chickpeas, super well-blended into the tehina sauce.

Same as It Ever Was

We arrive at Abu Michel, a hummusiya in the old city of Lod, a mixed Jewish-Arab town about ten miles from Tel Aviv. My father (Mordecai, but everyone calls him Solo) grew up a block away from here. As a kid, he'd come to Abu Michel on Mondays for a half portion of hummus on credit. On Fridays, when he got his allowance (about 30 cents), he'd return for the second half.

My father has been eating hummus at Abu Michel for going on sixty years and regards it as among the best in the country. I was less than two weeks old when I was here the first time, so I can't comment on how it's changed, but Solo swears that it tastes the same as ever. When he asks the owner, Michel Abu Tabit, how he has kept his hummus so consistently good for so many years, Michel answers with a straight face: "My father made a big batch before he died, and we keep it in the freezer." His eyes and mouth break into a wide, warm smile.

Michel has the quiet, gentle bearing of a favorite grandfather, belying the toughness required to sustain his restaurant in a place like Lod. He was just fourteen years old when he arranged the purchase of the restaurant on behalf of his father. The negotiations with the seller lasted about five minutes, during which time Michel's father didn't say a word. Michel quickly put his parents to work in the kitchen and set about stopping the brawling and

rambunctiousness for which the establishment had been known under previous owners.

Israelis tend to regard the town of Lod, if they regard it at all, as a run-down backwater. A majority of the original Arab residents either fled or were forced out in 1948, replaced by a succession of poor immigrants, lately dominated by Russians and Ethiopians. Lod was the second and final stop for my grandmother, Solo's mother, Savta Mati, after she arrived in Israel from Bulgaria. She lived here over fifty years, until her death.

For the last few decades, a thriving drug trade and the accompanying violence, along with government corruption, tensions between Arab and Jewish residents, and a lack of economic opportunity have cast the city in a negative light. Although there are some early signs of gentrification in Lod and Ramla, its neighbor to the south, it is nearby Ben Gurion

International Airport that has kept Lod on the map. Abu Michel has long been a favorite lunch spot for El Al employees (including my father) and was a popular meeting place for important military and political figures. Michel proudly tells us that the military commander and politician Moshe Dayan ate here most Thursdays and prime minister Golda Meir visited four times.

Abu Michel is also rumored to be the location where agents planned the kidnapping of Adolf Eichmann from Argentina to stand trial in Israel. In the Nelson DeMille novel *By the Rivers of Babylon*, a thriller about a Middle East peace mission, there are three mentions of the restaurant, says Michel.

Same as it ever was.

Abu Michel

LOD | Four members of Michel Abu Tabit's family, representing three generations, are working in the restaurant this afternoon. Our table is covered in salatim and bowls of hummus and a few ground kebabs for good measure. The specialty of the house, masabacha *(top center)* is particularly delicious. We use soft pita to scoop up the not-quite-warm chickpeas, dressed in rich tehina with lemon and olive oil.

Spice Blends and Sauces

While excellent prepared seasonings are now available at specialty stores, here's how to make your own. See Resources *(page 17)* for where to find unfamiliar ingredients.

Shawarma Spice Blend #1
for Red Meat
Makes about 1 cup

Combine ½ cup ground sumac, ¼ cup smoked paprika, 2 tablespoons garlic powder, 2 tablespoons onion powder, and 1 tablespoon cayenne in a small bowl and mix well. Store in a covered jar.

Shawarma Spice Blend #2
for Poultry
Makes about 1 cup

Combine ½ cup ground turmeric, ½ cup ground cumin, ½ cup ground black pepper, and 2 tablespoons each ground cardamom and ground coriander in a small bowl and mix well. Store in a covered jar.

Shawarma Spice Blend #3
for Vegetables
Makes about 1 cup

Combine ¼ cup each ground turmeric, ground cumin, ground fenugreek, and ground cinnamon with 1 tablespoon each ground allspice and ground black pepper in a small bowl and mix well. Store in a covered jar.

Hawaij Spice Blend
Makes ½ cup

Combine ¼ cup ground turmeric, 2 tablespoons freshly ground black pepper, and 2 tablespoons ground cumin in a small bowl and mix well. Store in a covered jar.

Fresh Harissa
North African Pepper Sauce
Makes about 3 cups

Combine 4 mildly hot chiles and 2 stemmed and seeded red bell peppers with 2 garlic cloves, 1 tablespoon kosher salt, 2 teaspoons ground cinnamon, and 1 teaspoon each ground coriander and ground caraway in a food processor and process until smooth. Taste and add olive oil and lemon juice. Keeps, covered and refrigerated, for up to 2 weeks.

Fermented Harissa
Makes about 3 cups

Combine 4 mildly hot chiles, 2 stemmed and seeded red bell peppers, 2 garlic cloves, 1 tablespoon kosher salt, 2 teaspoons ground cinnamon, and 1 teaspoon each ground coriander and ground caraway in a food processor and process until smooth. Transfer to a container, cover with plastic wrap, and keep at room temperature for 7 days. Taste and add olive oil and lemon juice. Keeps, covered and refrigerated, for up to 2 weeks.

Black Harissa
Black Garlic Chile Sauce
Makes about 1½ cups

Steep 4 ancho chiles in a bowl of hot water for 15 minutes. Drain well and remove the stems. Combine the chiles, 8 black garlic cloves, ½ cup ground Urfa pepper, ½ cup canola oil, 1 tablespoon kosher salt, and 1 tablespoon sherry vinegar in a food processor. Process until smooth. Taste and add more salt and vinegar if needed. Keeps, covered and refrigerated, for up to 2 weeks.

Peanut Harissa
Makes about 3 cups

Preheat the oven to 350°F. Toss 1 cup roasted, unsalted peanuts with 2 tablespoons canola oil and 2 teaspoons kosher salt, then spread them on a baking sheet and toast for 6 to 8 minutes, or until fragrant. Transfer the peanuts to a cutting board and let cool. Coarsely chop, then transfer to a bowl. Mix in 2 cups Fresh Harissa. Taste and add lemon juice and salt. Keeps, covered and refrigerated, for up to 1 week.

Merguez Spice Blend

Makes about 1 cup

Combine ¼ cup crushed Aleppo pepper, 2 tablespoons fennel seed, 2 tablespoons ground cumin, and 1 tablespoon each ground cardamom, caraway seeds, and coriander seeds in a spice grinder or mortar and pestle and grind to a powder. Store in a covered jar.

Muhammara

Red Bell Pepper Spread

Makes about 2 cups

Toast 1 cup walnuts. Roast, peel, and seed 4 red bell peppers. Combine the walnuts, peppers, 2 tablespoons paprika, and 2 tablespoons pomegranate molasses in a food processor and process until just smooth. Scoop the mixture into a bowl, taste, and add lemon juice, olive oil, and kosher salt. Keeps, covered and refrigerated, for up to 1 week.

Harif

Hot Sauce

Makes about 2 cups

Slice 2 onions into ½-inch-thick rounds and char them well on both sides on a grill or in a hot pan. Soak 2 or 3 dried spicy chiles and a couple of dried ancho chiles in hot water.for 10 minutes. Drain well and discard the stems. Place the charred onions and chiles in the bowl of a food processor and puree until very smooth. Taste and add olive oil, red wine vinegar, and kosher salt. Keeps, covered and refrigerated, for up to 2 weeks.

Everyday Schug

Makes about 2 cups

Combine ½ pound stemmed serrano chiles and 3 tablespoons kosher salt in a food processor and process until smooth. Transfer to a bowl and stir in 3 tablespoons lemon juice, 2 tablespoons canola oil, and 2 teaspoons ground coriander. Taste and add more salt if needed. Keeps, covered and refrigerated, for up to 3 weeks.

Hummus Toppings

Each of the 24 recipes that follow serves 4 atop a batch of 5-Minute Hummus. They're also great alone, hot or at room temperature, as salads, side dishes, or condiments. Top that!

In Israel and the Middle East, hummus is generally not considered to be a dish that needs improvement. After almost 1,000 years, people are pretty much OK with where hummus is at. It doesn't need to be deconstructed, or reconstructed; it doesn't benefit from being liquefied, gasified, atomized, homogenized, or clarified. Sure, you can put an egg on it. And yes, there are toppings, like foul (pronounced "fool"; it's the fava bean stew that originated in Egypt well before hummus arrived on the scene) and masabacha, cooked chickpeas swimming in tehina. But both of these dishes are eaten alone as often as they are used to top a bowl of hummus. With one or two exceptions, the canon of hummus toppings in Israel is sealed.

Fortunately, in America, our traditions aren't that old, and we believe that hummus makes an irresistible canvas for toppings. Great hummus is delicious all by itself, but it is an even better partner. Its nutty richness enhances almost everything and is never overwhelmed. A plate of hummus with apricots and pine nuts doesn't need more than a couple of ounces of ground beef seasoned with Turkish coffee to make a convincing dinner. And vegetarians and vegans can rejoice in a world where hummus topped with avocado and peanut harissa exists.

When we opened Dizengoff, we were afraid that people wouldn't get the concept of hummus as a meal.

Toppings were our secret weapon. Our opening chef, Emily Seaman, converted local produce into a daily menu that read like a harvest calendar. She changed toppings faster than we could update the menu board, establishing our own tradition that keeps customers coming back to discover what's new—and hoping to find old favorites.

The recipes that follow represent some of our most popular toppings from Dizengoff over the last few years, the ideas of hummus slingers past and present: Elaine Gardner, Henry Morgan, Leandra Bourdot, Lissadell Cohen-Serrins, Caitlin McMillan, and, of course, Emily.

We've written these recipes to be intentionally a bit imprecise; they're designed for you to improvise with whatever is good or in season or sitting in your vegetable drawer. Hummus is magic: It pairs with almost anything good!

Pan-Roasted and Pickled Eggplant *(page 171)* with pomegranate seeds and date molasses.

Tehina Chicken Salad

1. Roast a chicken (or buy a rotisserie chicken!), peel off and reserve the skin, and shred the meat. Mix the meat in a large bowl with 1 cup each minced celery and red onion, and toss in whatever other minced vegetables you have on hand. Add a handful of toasted nuts and dried fruits if you like. Toss the chicken salad with plenty of Quick Tehina Sauce *(page 145)*, lemon juice, kosher salt, olive oil, and your favorite herbs.

2. To make crispy skin for topping, heat an inch or so of canola oil to 350°F in a medium saucepan. Slice up a few pieces of the reserved chicken skin and fry, turning, until golden brown; drain on paper towels.

3. Make 2 hard-boiled eggs. Drizzle each serving of chicken salad with Black Harissa *(page 150)* and top with some crispy chicken skin and half a hard-boiled egg.

Saffron-Braised Chicken

1. Preheat the oven to 350°F. Mix together 2 tablespoons Hawaij Spice Blend *(page 150)* and 1 teaspoon ground allspice in a small bowl. Rub the mixture over 4 skinless, boneless chicken thighs and set aside at room temperature for at least an hour.

2. While the chicken cures, peel and chop 1 onion and 2 carrots. Mince 3 garlic cloves and chop 1 cup dried apricots. Heat 1 tablespoon canola oil in a large ovenproof skillet. Sear the chicken on both sides, then transfer to a plate. Toss the vegetables into the skillet, reduce the heat, and cook until the onion and garlic are soft, about 5 minutes. Stir in ½ cup tomato paste, deglaze the skillet with 2 cups chicken stock or water, and add the apricots and a hefty pinch of saffron. Return the chicken to the skillet, cover, and transfer to the oven.

3. Braise for 25 to 30 minutes, or until the chicken falls apart easily. Let the chicken cool, then shred it in the pan. Taste and add salt if needed.

Avocado
with Peanut Harissa

Pit and peel 2 ripe avocados. Fan each
avocado half in slices over the hummus
and top with a few spoonfuls of Peanut
Harissa *(page 150)*.

Roasted Butternut Squash

1. Preheat the oven to 450°F. Cut a butternut squash in half and scoop out the seeds. Rub the squash with canola oil, sprinkle with kosher salt, and put it on a parchment paper–lined baking sheet, flesh side down. Roast for about 1 hour or until tender. Let cool.

2. Meanwhile, mix together about 1 cup each halved red grapes and toasted pistachios in a large bowl. Season with lemon juice, olive oil, salt, and chopped fresh herbs. Set aside. When the squash has cooled, scoop the flesh into a colander lined with cheesecloth and mash it with a fork. Drain the squash for 10 minutes, then gather up the cheesecloth and squeeze out as much moisture as you can. Transfer the squash to a bowl. Stir in about 1 cup Quick Tehina Sauce *(page 145)*. Taste and add more lemon juice, pepper, salt, and tehina if needed. Top each serving of squash with a few spoonfuls of the grape-pistachio salad.

Matbucha with Egg

1. For this classic tomato and pepper sauce, core, seed, and chop 1 red bell pepper and 2½ pounds heirloom tomatoes. Chop 1 onion and thinly slice 3 garlic cloves. Heat 1 tablespoon canola oil in a skillet. Add the pepper, onion, garlic, and a big pinch of kosher salt. Cook until soft, about 15 minutes, then stir in the tomatoes. When the liquid comes to a simmer, reduce the heat to low and cook for 1½ to 2 hours, or until the mixture resembles a chunky tomato sauce. Taste and add salt, lemon juice, and olive oil.

2. Meanwhile, hard-boil 2 eggs. Top each serving of hummus with some Matbucha, then with half an egg.

Corn Salad

1. Shuck 4 ears corn and cut off the kernels into a large bowl. Finely chop 1 onion and thinly slice 3 garlic cloves. Heat 2 tablespoons canola oil in a skillet and add the onion, garlic, and a pinch of kosher salt. Cook the onion and garlic for about 5 minutes, add the corn kernels, and cook, stirring, for another 10 minutes or until tender. Let cool.

2. Meanwhile, finely chop 4 Persian cucumbers and 1 red onion. Cut 1 pint cherry tomatoes in half and chop 2 medium heirloom tomatoes. Drain and rinse 1 (15-ounce) can chickpeas. Combine the vegetables and chickpeas in a large bowl and toss with the cooled corn mixture and about 1 cup mixed chopped fresh parsley and cilantro. Taste and add olive oil, lemon juice, and salt.

Onion Petals

Weird as it may sound, raw onion is a traditional Israeli vehicle for eating hummus. We like to use a petal to scoop hummus and stuff it inside a torn piece of pita. Not all raw onions are created equal, though, and not everyone likes playing Russian roulette with their breath. We've found that a quick dunk in a pickling liquid of vinegar, ground sumac, and cold water helps soften and mellow the onion while retaining its crunch. (Add a pinch of sugar if your onion's not a sweet Vidalia.)

Halil

RAMLA | On a Saturday afternoon, the eager crowd at Halil overflows onto the narrow, brick-paved streets of the beautiful old town of Ramla, a city with a rich history that dates to the 700s CE. Inside, both Arabs and Jews gather at tables in a workaday setting, eating bowls of tehina-rich hummus, French fries, kebabs, and salatim.

Lima Beans with Tomato and Cinnamon

1. Blanch 3 cups fresh lima beans (from 2½ pounds pods) or frozen lima beans in heavily salted boiling water for 3 minutes, then immediately transfer to a bowl of ice water to lock in the color.

2. Chop 1 onion and mince 3 garlic cloves. Cook the onion and garlic in 2 tablespoons canola oil until soft, about 5 minutes. Stir in 1 teaspoon ground cinnamon. Cook for a minute or two, then add 1 (28-ounce) can crushed tomatoes. Cook the sauce for 5 to 10 minutes, stir in the lima beans, and cook for a few minutes more. Taste and add kosher salt, then top with a handful or two of chopped fresh parsley and a drizzle of olive oil.

Ground Chicken with Amba

1. Roughly chop the rind of 1 preserved lemon or Quick-Pickled Lemons *(page 201)*. Add 1 tablespoon honey and 2 tablespoons water and puree in a blender until smooth.

2. Heat 2 tablespoons canola oil in a large skillet and add 1 grated onion. Cook for a minute or two, then add 1 pound ground chicken and continue cooking, stirring, until the chicken is just cooked through. Add 2 tablespoons of the lemon sauce, ½ cup Classic Mango Amba *(page 79)* or store-bought, 2 cups crushed tomatoes, 1 tablespoon ground cinnamon, and 1 teaspoon grated fresh ginger. Cook for 10 to 15 minutes more, stirring to prevent burning. Top with chopped fresh cilantro and a handful of toasted pine nuts.

Japanese Eggplant with Muhammara

Slice 3 or 4 Japanese eggplants on the bias into 1-inch-thick pieces. Place them on a wire rack set inside a rimmed baking sheet, salt liberally on both sides, and drain at room temperature for 1 hour. Brush the eggplant slices lightly with oil and grill or broil until charred on both sides. Spoon Muhammara *(page 151)* on top of the hummus and add the charred eggplant and some minced parsley.

Salt-Roasted Kohlrabi with Garlic Chips

1. Preheat the oven to 375°F. Trim 6 kohlrabi bulbs and wet them under running water. Roll them in enough kosher salt to coat. Roast for 1 to 1½ hours, or until they're fork-tender. Remove the kohlrabi from the oven, let cool, brush off the salt, then peel and cut into large dice. Toss the diced kohlrabi with 2 tablespoons chopped preserved lemon, a pinch of salt, a drizzle of olive oil, a squeeze of fresh lemon, and crushed Aleppo pepper.

2. **FOR THE GARLIC CHIPS:** Peel a large garlic clove and slice very thin. Put the slices in a colander and set under cold running water for 10 minutes. Make a simple syrup by heating 1 cup water with 1 cup sugar, stirring until the sugar has completely dissolved. Add the garlic and let it cook in the syrup over low heat for 1 hour. Drain and set aside to cool. Heat 1 inch of canola oil to 350°F in a small pot and fry the garlic slices until they're golden brown. Immediately remove them from the oil, drain on paper towels, and sprinkle with kosher salt. Toss the garlic chips over the kohlrabi and top with fresh herbs.

Carrots with Dukkah

1. Preheat the oven to 400°F. Peel 6 to 8 medium carrots and slice on the diagonal into 1-inch-thick pieces. Transfer to a bowl and season with kosher salt, 2 teaspoons ground coriander, and 1 teaspoon paprika. Drizzle in enough canola oil to coat the carrots and toss well. Roast the carrots in the oven on a baking sheet for about 15 minutes, until they're charred and soft.

2. To make the dukkah, toast ¼ cup sesame seeds in a hot skillet. Remove from the heat and set aside to cool. Place 2 tablespoons coriander seeds in a small bowl and crack them with the back of a spoon or a pestle. Add ½ cup coarsely chopped pistachios and the sesame seeds and mix well. Top each serving of carrots with dukkah and a drizzle of olive oil.

Roasted Corn with Long Hots

Preheat the oven to 500°F. Shuck 4 ears corn. Cut 2 long hot peppers in half lengthwise and remove and discard the stems and connected seed pods. Line a baking sheet with parchment paper and roast the corn and peppers for 10 to 15 minutes, or until browned, turning them at 5 or 6 minutes. Cut the corn kernels off the cobs into a large bowl. Slice the peppers and toss them with the corn and 1 cup chopped mixed fresh parsley and cilantro. Taste and add olive oil, kosher salt, and lemon juice. Mix together ⅓ cup Classic Mango Amba *(page 79)* or store-bought and ⅔ cup tehina in a small bowl and drizzle a few spoonfuls on top of the corn salad.

Pickled Beets with Pistachios

1. Preheat the oven to 300°F. Scrub 1 pound golden or any other beets, put them in a pot, and cover with about 1 quart olive oil. Stir in ¼ cup white wine vinegar. Cover and bake for 2 to 3 hours, or until the beets are fork-tender. Remove from the oven and let the beets cool to room temperature in the liquid.

2. Remove the cooled beets from the liquid, rub off their skins with paper towels, chop them into bite-size pieces, and put them in a large bowl. Add kosher salt and more vinegar as needed, and serve topped with chopped pistachios.

Crispy Oyster Mushrooms

1. Preheat the oven to 350°F. Toss ¼ cup pine nuts with a drizzle of canola oil and a pinch of kosher salt on a baking sheet. Toast for 5 to 10 minutes, or until golden brown. Remove from the oven and set aside.

2. Stem 1½ pounds oyster mushrooms. Heat a large skillet over medium-high heat. When the pan is very hot, add 2 tablespoons canola oil, then the mushrooms. Cook, undisturbed, for about 2 minutes, then sprinkle with 1 teaspoon salt and toss. Cook for another 2 minutes without stirring, add 1 tablespoon Shawarma Spice #3 *(page 150)*, and toss well. Remove from the heat, add 2 tablespoons sherry vinegar, and swirl the skillet. Return to the heat and cook until the liquid has evaporated, about 1 minute. Serve topped with toasted pine nuts and a drizzle of Quick Tehina Sauce *(page 145)*.

Charred Zucchini with Mint

Preheat a grill or broiler to high. Cut 3 medium zucchini in half lengthwise and toss with canola oil, kosher salt, and ground sumac. Grill or broil the zucchini until charred but still firm. Let cool, then cut each piece in half again lengthwise and chop into ½-inch chunks. Toss the zucchini in a large bowl with a cup or two of halved cherry tomatoes and 1 cup torn fresh mint leaves. Taste and add lemon juice, olive oil, salt, and ground sumac.

Broccoli and Pine Nut Pesto

1. Cut a large head of broccoli into bite-size florets. Peel the stems and chop into small pieces. Bring a large saucepan of salted water to a boil. Fill a bowl with ice water. Drop the chopped stems and all but 1 cup of the florets into the boiling water and cook for 1 minute, then immediately drain and transfer to the ice water.

2. Combine the blanched broccoli with about the same amount of toasted pine nuts in a food processor. Pulse a few times, then add ⅓ cup olive oil and process until smooth. Scoop the pesto into a bowl. Taste and add kosher salt and lemon juice.

3. Get a skillet really hot. Toss the reserved raw broccoli florets with 2 tablespoons canola oil, a couple of big pinches of crushed Aleppo pepper, and one pinch each of paprika, ground coriander, and salt in a small bowl. Transfer the seasoned florets to the hot skillet and sauté until browned and just tender. Top the pesto with the sautéed broccoli florets.

Braised Cabbage with Amba

Cut half a Napa cabbage into 6 wedges, then cut crosswise to make 1-inch squares. Finely chop 1 onion and mince 3 garlic cloves. Cook the onion and garlic in 2 tablespoons olive oil in a large skillet with a couple of pinches of kosher salt. When the onion is soft, add a pint of multicolored cherry tomatoes. Cook over medium heat for 15 to 20 minutes, or until the tomato skins pop and release their juices. Stir in the cabbage, reduce the heat to low, and cook, uncovered, for 20 to 30 minutes, adding a little water if the mixture looks dry. The cabbage should be very tender. Remove the pan from the heat and stir in up to ¼ cup Classic Mango Amba *(page 79)* or store-bought. Taste and add salt. Top with a drizzle of olive oil and a handful of chopped fresh parsley.

Black-Eyed Peas

1. Soak 2 cups dried black-eyed peas in water overnight. The next day, chop 2 onions and mince 4 garlic cloves. Smash 1 or 2 dried limes with the side of a knife, then buzz them in a spice grinder.

2. Cook the onions and garlic in 2 tablespoons canola oil in a large pot until soft, about 5 minutes. Add the ground limes and 1 tablespoon ground turmeric. Cook for a minute or two, then drain the beans and add them to the pot. Pour in enough cold water to cover the beans by an inch or two. Bring to a simmer and cook for 45 minutes to 1 hour, or until the beans are tender. Drain and season with kosher salt. Top with a handful of chopped fresh dill or parsley.

Chef Osama Dalal points out his grandmother's window, thirty feet above the Mediterranean. As a child, Osama would catch crab, spiny lobster, and cuttlefish by hand and put them in the basket his grandmother would lower from that window. Then she'd cook his catch.

Osama Dalal

AKKO | Osama Dalal's family has lived in Akko for more than 300 years. As a chef, Osama has championed the unique cuisine of his city, a product of its seaside location along the Silk Road (Marco Polo was here!). He takes us to Hummus El Abed Abu Hamid, *above right*, where we eat *thridi*, an ancient dish not found anywhere else in Israel. It is a unique mixture of pita, broth, chickpeas, and yogurt, reputed to be a favorite of the Prophet Muhammad.

An ambassador of authenticity, Osama demonstrates how Ottoman influences flavor the food of Akko, more than elsewhere in Israel. "People here are so connected to the emotions of the city," he says. "They cook not just for survival, but for happiness."

Lamb Meatballs

1. Preheat the oven to 450°F. Grate half an onion and 2 garlic cloves into a large bowl. Add 1 pound ground lamb, ¼ cup each chopped fresh cilantro and parsley, 2 teaspoons kosher salt, and 1 tablespoon Merguez Spice Blend *(page 151)*. Mix with your hands until just combined, then add ¼ cup seltzer and mix again. Make golf ball–size meatballs, place on a parchment paper–lined baking sheet, and roast for 5 minutes.

2. To make the sauce, cook 1 diced onion and 3 minced garlic cloves in canola oil with a pinch or two of kosher salt until the onion is soft, about 5 minutes. Whisk in ¼ cup tomato paste and 2 cups pomegranate juice and cook over medium-low heat, stirring, for 15 minutes. Add the meatballs and cook for 10 more minutes, or until they're cooked through. Top with fresh dill.

Ground Beef with Turkish Coffee

1. Heat 2 tablespoons canola oil in a medium skillet. Add 1 chopped onion, a few thinly sliced garlic cloves, and 1 pound ground beef. Season with 2 tablespoons Turkish coffee, 1 teaspoon ground Urfa pepper, 1 teaspoon ground sumac, ½ teaspoon ground allspice, and ¼ teaspoon ground cardamom.

2. Cook, breaking up the meat with a spatula, until the beef is browned. Fold in ½ cup chopped dried apricots. Taste for salt, and top with a handful of toasted pine nuts and fresh herbs.

Pan-Roasted and Pickled Eggplant

1. Peel 1 large eggplant and thickly slice crosswise. Salt each slice well on both sides and place on a wire rack on a rimmed baking sheet. Refrigerate overnight.

2. Dice 1 red bell pepper and 1 small onion. Heat a large skillet with 2 tablespoons canola oil and char the eggplant slices for 3 to 5 minutes on each side. Set aside. In the same skillet, heat 2 more tablespoons canola oil. Add the pepper, onion, and a pinch of kosher salt and cook until soft, about 5 minutes. Stir in the eggplant and deglaze with 3 tablespoons sherry vinegar. Mix well and remove from the heat.

3. Cool the eggplant mixture, then mix in 1 cup Quick Tehina Sauce *(page 145)*. Add generous handfuls of chopped fresh parsley and mint leaves. Taste and add salt and vinegar if needed. Top with pomegranate seeds and a drizzle of date molasses.

Pan-Roasted Green Beans

1. Trim about 3 cups green beans into 1-inch pieces. Chop 1 onion and mince 3 garlic cloves. Cook the onion and garlic in 2 tablespoons canola oil in a large skillet until the onion is soft, about 5 minutes. Add the green beans, 2 tablespoons crushed Aleppo pepper, and a pinch or two of kosher salt.

2. Cook, stirring frequently, for 8 to 10 minutes, or until the green beans are browned and just tender. Add ½ cup sliced almonds and cook another minute. Taste for salt.

Pan-Roasted Turnips with Dates and Harif

1. Trim and halve about 12 baby turnips. Transfer to a large bowl and toss with canola oil, kosher salt, and a pinch of ground Urfa pepper. Get a large skillet really hot, add the turnips, and roast them, stirring frequently, until they're charred on the outside and just tender. Cool the turnips.

2. Pit and thinly slice a handful of Medjool dates. Place them in a large bowl with some chopped fresh dill and minced red onion. Taste and add sherry vinegar, olive oil, and salt. Add the turnips and toss. Add 2 tablespoons (or more!) Harif *(page 150)* and toss again.

Charred Asparagus with Hazelnut Dukkah

1. To make the dukkah, toast ½ cup skinned hazelnuts in a hot skillet and transfer to a food processor. Add 1 tablespoon crushed Aleppo pepper, 1½ teaspoons sesame seeds, ½ teaspoon kosher salt, and the grated zest of ½ lemon. Pulse just until the hazelnuts are coarsely chopped.

2. Preheat the broiler. Trim 2 bunches asparagus and cut the spears on the diagonal into 1½-inch-long pieces. Place on a baking sheet and toss with canola oil and kosher salt. Broil until the asparagus is charred but still crisp, watching it closely and tossing every few minutes. Top the asparagus with a scattering of dukkah, a drizzle of olive oil, and some chopped fresh dill.

CHAPTER 9
Salads

A wise man once said, "You don't win friends with salad." He obviously hadn't been to Israel yet.

In less than a century, Jewish immigrants became the majority population of one of the oldest inhabited pieces of land on earth. They came to Israel from all over the world: North Africa, the Arabian Peninsula, the Levant, the Balkans and the rest of Europe, and Central Asia. They represented literally dozens of cultures, each with its own food traditions. And they set their tables in a place with a well-worn food culture of its own. The fact that so many disparate cultures coalesced into a unified cuisine is as absurd as it is true. And I think it has something to do with salad.

Here in America, we often think of salad the way Allen Iverson thinks about practice: It's the thing that comes before the thing that counts. Forget the triple-washed greens and bottled dressing. Bring on the meat. In Israel, salad is practically the whole ball game. The mountains of chopped vegetables at every falafel or shawarma stand in the country are the secret ingredients that make those iconic sandwiches sing. Even breakfast comes with salad.

And certainly no table is complete without an array of vegetable-centric salads—salatim—to begin the meal. It is a regional tradition born of ecomony,

Previous spread: In Jerusalem's Machane Yehuda Market, tomatoes and cucumbers destined to become Israeli salad. *This page:* At Maayan haBira in Haifa, a dozen salads welcome guests.

Salads greet us at the Libyan restaurant Guetta in Tel Aviv: preserved lemons, pickled white cabbage, spicy carrot salad, and our favorite, the squash salad chirshi *(page 196)*, *bottom left*.

hospitality, and pure joy. And it is a tradition that was enthusiastically adapted by Jewish immigrants arriving from all over the world. A Romanian family may start a meal with different salatim than an Iraqi family, but rest assured that both meals will begin with salads.

Nowhere is this more evident than in the unassuming family restaurants, storefront grills, and humble workingmen's cafés that are the heart and soul of Israeli food outside of the home. To sit down at one of these establishments is to hear a little bit of the story of Israel.

Itzik HaGadol

JAFFA | Founded in 1996, this quintessential *shipudiya* (Israeli grill) is more polished than the average joint. An impressive array of salatim, like the griddled eggplant *above*, precedes the main event: succulent cuts of charcoal-grilled beef, lamb, and poultry, plus special bits like spinal cord, spleen, and even testicles.

At **Morris Restaurant**, the boisterous grill in Jerusalem's Machane Yehuda Market that comes to life after the produce merchants have sold their last eggplant for the day, the salatim are served in disposable plastic bowls. The Morris brothers—first-generation Israelis via Morocco—serve salatim that are basic, almost remedial: pickled beets, Moroccan carrots, lightly dressed shredded cabbage, chopped salad. But they are well seasoned and vivid from vegetables that were in the ground only a day or two ago. Along with plates of hummus and baskets of pita, the salads are a bright counterpoint to the parade of juicy grilled meats dripping with fat that follows.

At **Al Ein**, the Druze restaurant in the Galilee, the salatim incorporate wild plants foraged from the verdant, fertile hills of northern Israel. Chicory is stewed in olive oil, and akkoub, a member of the thistle family known in the U.S. as gundelia, is cooked with chickpeas and lemon.

At **Haj Kahil**, the Arabic restaurant on the main traffic circle entering Jaffa, mounds of chopped dill dressed with olive oil and lemon and enlivened by sour cherries and almonds are a classic but unexpected delight. A salad of cactus fruit with mint and marinated labneh cheese is a modern creation that is perfectly at home in this Arabic kitchen.

The table at **Guetta**, a restaurant in Tel Aviv specializing in the Jewish cuisine of Tripoli, would not be complete without chirshi, the condiment-slash-salad that will forever change how you think about winter squash.

You could eat for days at Itzik HaGadol ("Big Isaac's") in Jaffa, and we did. And this is just the salad course!

Al Ein

EIN AL-ASSAD | Before Abu Samach opened a small restaurant in his home in the Druze village of Ein al-Assad, he worked in prison logistics. His wife runs the kitchen, and her cooking showcases the bountiful produce of the Galilee. Some locally grown surprises, like succulent thistle, mallow, and chicory, are foraged from the hillsides. Hospitality is an abundance of plates.

Salad is both a common denominator of Israeli cuisine and a celebration of its diversity.

At **Yonak** *(page 213)*, a Romanian restaurant in Haifa, the salatim spread reflects its European influence: eggplant with tons of garlic, and plates of pleasantly effervescent pickled whole tomatoes and cucumbers. Across town at **Maayan haBira** *(page 208)*, a Polish grill and tap house, a similar salatim spread also includes two kinds of preserved herring; chrain, a sinus-clearing salad of grated beets and horseradish; and slices of pickled watermelon.

Just a few miles south of the border with Lebanon, at **Artzim**, a Lebanese restaurant, the tabbouleh is composed almost entirely of parsley with a touch of bulgur. Fattoush, the Levantine bread salad, combines leftover toasted pita chips with chopped vegetables, plenty of olive oil, and lemon juice for a particularly luscious and satisfying dish.

The iconic grill **Itzik HaGadol** (literally, "Big Isaac's") in Jaffa puts out the most impressive salad spread of all, including no fewer than eighteen items spanning the cultural range of Israel: four different eggplant preparations from four different traditions; schmaltzy European-style chopped liver; grated carrots with chiles and preserved lemon; Turkish salad with scallions.

An array of bright, fresh, and flavorful salads is a remarkably compelling way to eat, particularly at a moment when plant-based diets are gaining currency. The sheer variety of salads on Israeli tables stimulates the eyes and the appetite. And for those of us who still enjoy a nice piece of animal protein, beginning a meal with salatim reduces our consumption and brings balance to the universe.

In this chapter, we've included eighteen of our favorite salatim recipes, beginning with Eight Quick Essential Salads that, with a little advance planning, can be prepared in under twenty minutes. It's not unreasonable to think that you could put a spread of salatim on the table in the time it takes to roast a chicken or steam some rice. All of them can be made ahead and stored in the refrigerator until you're ready to sit down.

A spread of salads is a no-brainer for entertaining. The simple act of passing little dishes back and forth across the table is guaranteed to turn strangers into friends. See Resources *(page 17)* for where to find unfamiliar ingredients.

Cabbage with Onion, Sumac, and Dill

Grated Carrots with Chiles

Roasted Eggplant with Peppers

Matbucha

Abe Fisher Beet Salad

Chopped Salad

Turkish Salad

Radish and Zucchini Salad
with Mint and Nigella Seeds

Turkish Salad
Serves 4

1. Core, seed, and chop 3 red bell peppers. Chop 2 onions. Thinly slice 4 garlic cloves. Slice a bunch of scallions on the bias. Sauté the peppers with 1 tablespoon kosher salt and ¼ cup canola oil in a large skillet until soft, about 4 minutes. Add the onions and garlic. Cook until the onions are translucent, about 10 minutes.

2. Fold in 1 pint halved cherry tomatoes. Add 2 teaspoons smoked paprika and 2 teaspoons ground coriander and toast the spices for about 2 minutes. Transfer to a bowl, add the sliced scallions, taste, and add a pinch of salt, a squeeze of lemon juice, and a drizzle of olive oil.

Radish and Zucchini Salad with Mint and Nigella Seeds
Serves 4

Slice 1 bunch radishes, grate 2 medium zucchini, and chop a handful of fresh mint leaves. Mix together in a medium bowl with 1 tablespoon nigella seeds. Taste and add a pinch of kosher salt, a squeeze of lemon juice, and a few drops of olive oil.

Chopped Salad

Serves 4

Chop 5 Persian cucumbers and 3 heirloom
tomatoes. Finely chop 1 small red onion
and small handfuls of fresh dill, mint, and
parsley. Mix together in a large bowl.
Taste and add a pinch of kosher salt.
Dress generously with olive oil
and lemon juice.

Grated Carrots with Chiles

Serves 4

1. Stem, seed, and thinly slice 1 mild chile (like Fresno) and 1 serrano chile. Mix the chiles in a small bowl with 2 teaspoons kosher salt and 1 teaspoon sugar. Marinate at room temperature for at least 1 hour. Separately, make the Quick Pickled Lemons *(page 201)*.

2. Peel and grate 3 large carrots. Put the carrots in a bowl and add the chiles, pickled lemon slices, and 2 tablespoons olive oil. Mix well, taste, and add salt, a squeeze of lemon juice, and a drop more olive oil. Arrange on a plate and top with chopped fresh cilantro.

Matbucha
Moroccan Cooked Tomato-and-Pepper Salad
Serves 4

Core, seed, and finely chop a red bell pepper. Finely chop 1 onion. Thinly slice 3 garlic cloves. Quarter 8 plum tomatoes. Sauté the pepper, onion, and garlic in a large saucepan with 1 tablespoon kosher salt and ¼ cup canola oil. When the vegetables are translucent, about 15 minutes, add the tomatoes. Cook for 1 to 1½ hours, or until the mixture resembles a chunky tomato sauce. Transfer to a bowl, taste, and add salt, a squeeze of lemon juice, and a drizzle of olive oil. Scatter cilantro leaves on top.

Cabbage with Onion, Sumac, and Dill
Serves 4

1. Halve and core 1 head Napa cabbage and chop into 1-inch squares. Put the cabbage in a heatproof bowl. Mix 1½ cups distilled white vinegar, 1 cup water, ½ cup sugar, and ¼ cup kosher salt in a medium saucepan. Bring to a boil, stirring to completely dissolve the sugar and salt. Pour the hot liquid over the cabbage. Cover, let cool to room temperature, then marinate for at least an hour, or in the refrigerator for up to 2 days.

2. An hour before serving, finely chop 1 red onion. Toss in a bowl with 2 tablespoons ground sumac and 1 tablespoon salt. Marinate at room temperature for at least 1 hour, tossing frequently. Drain the cabbage and onion and mix together in a bowl. Add chopped fresh dill. Taste and add a pinch of salt, a squeeze of lemon juice, and a drizzle of olive oil.

Abe Fisher Beet Salad

Serves 4

1. Preheat the oven to 375°F. Scrub 2 large beets; remove the greens. Layer 1 cup kosher salt in a small baking dish. Place the beets on the salt and cover the dish tightly with foil. Bake until fork-tender, about 1 hour. Remove the beets from the oven, let cool, peel with paper towels, and shred on the coarse holes of a box grater. Transfer to a bowl.

2. Process 1 cup peeled, chopped fresh horseradish, 2 cups white vinegar, ½ cup apple cider vinegar, 1 tablespoon salt, and 1 tablespoon sugar in a food processor until smooth.

Add this mixture to the beets, cover, and marinate overnight at room temperature.

3. The next day, drain the beets in a colander set over a bowl. Reserve the horseradish-beet vinegar to pickle turnips or use in vinaigrette. Toss the marinated beets with 1 tablespoon olive oil, 2 teaspoons Dijon mustard, 1 minced shallot, and chopped fresh dill and parsley. Scatter more grated horseradish on top.

Roasted Eggplant with Peppers

Serves 4

Preheat a grill or broiler. Rub 1 large eggplant with canola oil and kosher salt. Grill or broil it whole for about 20 minutes per side, or until soft and cooked through. Let cool. Meanwhile, mix 1½ teaspoons kosher salt and ¼ cup red wine vinegar in a medium bowl. Core, seed, and finely chop a red and a green bell pepper. Finely chop 1 small red onion. Thinly slice 3 garlic cloves. Add the vegetables to the bowl, mix well, and marinate at room temperature for at least 30 minutes or up to 2 hours. Drain. Halve the eggplant, scoop out the flesh, and chop it. Add to the bowl and mix well. Arrange on a plate and top with chopped fresh parsley.

Sitting down to a table of twelve to twenty carefully prepared dishes inspired us to create our own version: Eight Quick Essential Salads *(page 184).*

Fattoush with Corn
Lebanese Salad with Crispy Pita
Serves 4

Preheat the oven to 350°F. Cut 2 fresh pitas into bite-size pieces. Toss with kosher salt and canola oil and toast until golden brown and crispy. Finely chop 1 red bell pepper, half a red onion, 4 Persian cucumbers, and 2 large tomatoes. Chop 1 head Bibb lettuce. Put the vegetables in a large bowl, add the toasted pita, 1 tablespoon kosher salt, 2 tablespoons lemon juice, 2 tablespoons olive oil, ½ cup corn kernels, and a handful of chopped fresh herbs. Mix well.

Dill Tabbouleh

Serves 4

Bring 1 cup water to a simmer and pour over
½ cup bulgur in a heatproof bowl. Add a pinch
of kosher salt. Cover tightly with plastic wrap; let
the bulgur bloom for 30 minutes. Chop 2 cups
fresh dill sprigs and finely chop half a red onion.
Fluff the bulgur with a fork and add the dill,
onion, 2 tablespoons lemon juice, 2 tablespoons
olive oil, and 1 teaspoon salt. Mix well, taste,
and add more salt, lemon juice, and olive oil
as needed.

Mofarket Al Abed

Egg Salad from Akko

Serves 4

Hard-boil and peel 4 eggs. Finely chop a red
onion and a small handful of parsley. Heat
1 tablespoon oil in a skillet, add the onion and a
pinch of kosher salt, and cook until translucent,
about 5 minutes. Add 1 tablespoon baharat and
toast for another minute. Let cool. Combine the
eggs, onion mixture, parsley, and 1 tablespoon
olive oil in a medium bowl. Mix well, mashing
the eggs. Taste and add a pinch of salt, a
squeeze of lemon juice, a drizzle
of olive oil, and some fresh
parsley leaves.

Chirshi
Libyan Squash Salad
Serves 4

1. Preheat the oven to 350°F. Finely chop 1 small onion and 1 red bell pepper. Thinly slice 2 garlic cloves. Cook the onion and garlic in a couple of tablespoons of canola oil with a pinch of kosher salt until soft, about 5 minutes. Add the pepper and cook over medium-low heat for about 15 minutes, until the vegetables are soft. Add 1 tablespoon smoked paprika and toast for another 30 seconds, until fragrant. Remove from the heat.

2. Cut a butternut squash in half lengthwise and scoop out the seeds. Cut off about ¼ cup squash to pickle later. Season the remaining squash with canola oil and few pinches of salt. Roast on a baking sheet for about 45 minutes, or until fork-tender. Let cool. Cut the reserved raw squash into small pieces and finely chop the rind of 2 lemons and place in a heatproof medium bowl. Combine 1 cup white wine vinegar, ⅔ cup water, and ⅓ cup sugar in a small saucepan.

Bring to a boil, stirring to dissolve the sugar, then pour the brine over the squash and lemon rind. Set aside to pickle at room temperature for at least 1 hour or up to overnight.

3. Scoop the roasted butternut flesh into a large bowl and add the onion-pepper mixture, 2 teaspoons ground coriander, and the pickled squash and lemon rind. Mix together, taste, and add salt and lemon juice as needed.

Carrot Chrain
Serves 4

Peel 2 large carrots and grate on the coarse holes of a box grater. Heat 1 tablespoon olive oil in a medium skillet over medium-high heat. Add the carrots and a pinch of kosher salt and cook until softened. Transfer to a bowl. Add ¼ cup prepared horseradish, 1 teaspoon sugar, and 1 teaspoon Dijon mustard. Mix well, taste, and add more salt and up to 2 more tablespoons horseradish if you like.

Can you imagine the size of the whole squash? Huge hunks are sold in the Machane Yehuda Market in Jerusalem.

Mshawashe
Arabic Bean Salad
Serves 4

Soak 1 cup dried fava beans and 1 cup
dried chickpeas overnight in 2 cups water
with a pinch of baking soda in separate
bowls. The next day, drain the beans, put
them in separate pots, and cover with
fresh water. Cook, covered, over medium
heat until the beans are soft and creamy
on the inside. (The chickpeas will take
about 2 hours, the favas about 3 hours.)
Drain and transfer the cooked beans
to a large bowl. Mash with the back
of a spoon and add ½ cup Quick
Tehina Sauce *(page 145)*,
2 tablespoons lemon juice,
2 tablespoons olive
oil, and 1 teaspoon
kosher salt. Taste
and adjust
seasonings as
needed.

Turkish Eggplant

Serves 4

1. Finely chop 1 red bell pepper and 1 onion. Thinly slice 2 mildly hot chiles and 3 garlic cloves. Cook the vegetables in a medium pot with 2 tablespoons canola oil until translucent, about 15 minutes. Add 1 (32-ounce) can crushed tomatoes. Cook until the liquid has reduced by about half, about 40 minutes. Remove from the heat.

2. Stripe 4 Japanese eggplants lengthwise with a vegetable peeler and cut on the diagonal into 2-inch-thick slices. Sprinkle the slices liberally on both sides with kosher salt. Transfer to a rack on a rimmed baking sheet to drain at room temperature for at least 30 minutes or up to 2 hours.

3. To make the salad, place a cast-iron skillet over medium-high heat. Sear the eggplant pieces on each side, then transfer to a plate and top with the cooked vegetables and a pinch of salt.

Chickpeas with Baharat, Tomatoes, and Brown Butter

Serves 4

Cook 5 tablespoons salted butter in a small saucepan over medium heat until it turns brown, about 2 minutes. Chop 2 large tomatoes. Drain and rinse 1 (15-ounce) can chickpeas. Combine the tomatoes and chickpeas in a medium bowl. Strain the brown butter through a fine sieve over the tomatoes and chickpeas. Toss well. Taste and add a pinch of kosher salt and a squeeze of lemon juice.

Quick Pickled Lemons

Makes 1½ to 2 cups

Scrub 2 lemons, then cut into quarters and slice as thinly as you can. Transfer to a bowl and add 2 tablespoons kosher salt and 2 tablespoons sugar. Toss well, cover, and let macerate at room temperature for at least 2 hours and up to 6 hours. Mix in 1 tablespoon olive oil. The lemons will keep in a covered container in the refrigerator for 2 weeks.

Pickled Watermelon

Makes 1 watermelon

Thinly slice 1 red seedless watermelon, then cut each slice into smaller pieces. Combine 1½ cups red wine vinegar, 1 cup water, 1 cup sugar, and 2 tablespoons kosher salt in a deep covered container. Mix to dissolve the sugar and salt.

Submerge the watermelon in the brine, cover, and pickle at room temperature for 2 hours or in the refrigerator for 4 to 6 hours. They'll keep, refrigerated, up to 1 week.

AT THE TABLE

CHAPTER 10

Ashkenazi

"So how did Israeli food end up mostly Sephardic? Is it just better?"

Steve and I both grew up in Ashkenazi households. Although my father is Israeli, my mother's family was from Ohio, via Lithuania. Steve is a descendant of prewar immigrants from Lithuania and Russia. Today, Ashkenazi Jews (those of European ancestry) represent about 75 percent of world Jewry, with a vast majority living in the United States. The Jewish food we're familiar with here was adapted from the Ashkenazi canon—Polish, Hungarian, Russian, German—mostly a peasant cuisine, but one that arrived in America before the devastation of the Holocaust. In the melting pot of early twentieth-century America, the great industrial cities produced a rich Jewish-American cuisine, awash in delicious stereotypes like pastrami, gefilte fish, chopped liver, and egg creams.

By the late nineteenth century, a Zionist movement emerged; Ashkenazi Jews were increasingly drawn to what was then Palestine, and would be crucial in making the state of Israel. Ashkenazi Jews dominated the Jewish state in its infancy and controlled the country's intellectual, cultural, and political institutions long after they no longer made up a majority of the population.

But when it came to cuisine, things went down differently. Mostly, the country's climate was incompatible with the staple crops of Europe. This

Previous spread: Appetizers at the wildly busy Maayan haBira, an Eastern European beer hall in Haifa. *This page:* Food writer Adeena Sussman's favorite smoked–fish monger at Merkaz HaDagim, in Tel Aviv.

Itzik and Ruti

TEL AVIV | This impossibly narrow storefront has been serving zaftig sandwiches since 1957—fried eggs with mayonnaise, hot dogs with sauerkraut, tuna salad—all on fresh European-style loaves. (Of course, nothing is immune to the Sephardic hegemony; their shakshouka sandwich is one of the shop's bestsellers.) The first sandwiches go out before 5 a.m., a reflection of the neighborhood's working-class roots. Itzik and Ruti have been replaced by their son Dudi and his wife, Shuli, but the crowds have not let up. The shop starts running out of things throughout the morning until it closes just before lunch. It's a heckuva business model.

You can still find a few old-school haunts that harken back to Israel's early Ashkenazi days.

reality, coupled with severe economic austerity during Israel's formative years, made for a poor representation of Ashkenazi cooking in that fledgling country. But there was also a strong ideological motivation to leave the old country behind altogether. The Zionist movement was built on the ideal of a strong, self-sufficient Jewish people, breaking the millennia-old cycle of persecution and exile.

The culinary traditions of the Holocaust-devastated European Jewry would not advance this fresh image. On the other hand, the indigenous cuisine that early Jewish pioneers encountered in Palestine fit the bill perfectly. It didn't hurt that Mizrahi immigrants (mostly from the Middle East) and Sephardic immigrants (mostly from the Iberian Peninsula and North Africa, who were beginning to outnumber the Ashkenazi) brought similar or overlapping cuisines that were already Jewish. Taken together, this food was Eastern and exotic and exuberant—everything the old (read: Ashkenazi) country was not.

And so Sephardic food won the hearts and minds of the nation and became virtually synonymous with Israeli food. But there has always been Ashkenazi cuisine in Israel. Much of what remains today can be found in the Hassidic community, descendants of a spiritual revival movement from eighteenth-century Eastern Europe. Much of the Hassidic way of life is frozen in time from this period, effectively preserving Ashkenazi culinary traditions, from kugels to knaidlach, as they existed in prewar Europe. But these foods are not often found in Israeli restaurants, and the best examples are largely hidden from public view.

Mati Bar, in a quiet corner of Levinsky Market in Tel Aviv, is a monument to the underappreciated charms of Ashkenazi food. The place has been a draft beer destination since 1973, perfect for washing down salty pickles, cured sardines, and salami. What it lacks in ambience, it more than makes up for in indifferent service. One gets the sense that to be welcomed here as a regular is a hard-won accomplishment. The bar's few interior tables are often occupied by old men arguing politics over plates of pickled herring and chopped liver. As these *alte kakers* (Yiddish for "old farts") die off, the taste for this food (and the knowledge of how to prepare it) is at risk of being buried with them.

The Holocaust forever cut off Ashkenazi cuisine from its European headwaters, and its vitality is now dependent on Jewish communities outside of Israel. Fortunately, a revival is underway. Throughout the U.S. the trend among young cooks to explore their ethnic roots has stimulated them to revisit bagels, the delicatessen, the appetizing store, and the bakery in the context of the artisanal ethos of the day.

To reimagine the flavors of our childhoods, we, along with our partner, chef Yehuda Sichel, opened **Abe Fisher** *(page 220)* on Sansom Street in Philadelphia in 2014. The restaurant is named after a fictional man—a mensch who grew up on New York's Lower East Side just as Jewish-American food was beginning to coalesce into a recognizable cuisine. Abe Fisher explores the food of our grandparents in an updated cultural exchange with melting-pot America. The menu offers the unexpected: schnitzel tacos, borscht tartare (made with pickled beets), and fish cured with gin. There is chicken liver mousse, smooth and rich enough to please both a French chef and a Jewish grandmother, and the whole roast duck combines Hungarian-Jewish tradition with our childhood memories of Chinatown Peking duck.

Ashkenazi food may never win a swimsuit competition with Sephardic food, the new poster child for the Mediterranean diet. But what does Sephardic cuisine have that can outduel a pastrami sandwich?

Maayan haBira

HAIFA | Mayaan haBira literally translates to "Fountain of Beer," and the crowd at this Haifa landmark appears to be taking this to heart on a midweek summer night. Indoor tables are jam-packed, but the real action is outside. In front of the restaurant the street is blocked off, more or less permanently, to accommodate the hundreds of guests who gather at this beer garden–meets–deli–meets–barbecue joint near Israel's largest port.

The restaurant was opened in 1962 by Nahum Meir, a Polish immigrant who was previously employed on the premises when it was a butcher shop and sausage factory. Mayaan haBira is now in its third generation of family stewardship and is as busy as ever.

Chicken Liver Mousse

Serves 4

GRIBENES

- 2 onions, sliced
- ½ cup raw chicken skins (from a whole chicken)
- ¼ cup rendered chicken fat (schmaltz) or vegetable oil
- 1 tablespoon sherry vinegar

CHICKEN LIVERS

- 1 pound chicken livers
- 1 tablespoon kosher salt
- 1 tablespoon ground caraway
- ¼ cup sherry vinegar

CHICKEN LIVER MOUSSE

- 4 onions, thinly sliced, caramelized in schmaltz or canola oil *(see page 126)*
- 2 hard-boiled eggs
- ¼ cup chicken stock
- Kosher salt
- Toasted Rye Bread *(page 218)* or other thin toast

Ashkenazi Jews' affinity for chopped liver is connected to their historic reliance on goose fat (or schmaltz) as a primary cooking fat. This was especially true in Northern Europe, where olive oil was unavailable and pork fat was the choice for much of the population.

The liver was merely a by-product that was not to be wasted. And what a by-product it was! For centuries Jews were the keepers of the controversial secrets behind foie gras, the fattened livers of geese and ducks.

In Eastern Europe the more plebeian chicken (and their livers) predominated. Because the liver is an organ that filters blood, the only way to make it kosher is to broil it to death. This only accentuates its metallic and bitter flavor components and fuels the rhetoric of liver haters everywhere. To combat this propaganda, Jewish cooks mixed the coarsely chopped livers with hard-boiled eggs and sautéed onions, which added the balance of fat and sweetness and stretched the dish to feed more ungrateful complainers.

Our version takes chopped liver into another realm, with the addition of deeply caramelized onions, rendered chicken skins (gribenes), and a healthy dose of schmaltz (or vegetable oil), all pureed together until perfectly smooth. The result is a creamy, impossibly light mousse that might even win over a few converts from the anti-liver establishment.

1. MAKE THE GRIBENES: Place the onions, chicken skins, and chicken fat or oil in a pot small enough that the onions are piled about 3 inches high. Cook on medium-low heat for 30 minutes, stirring occasionally, then reduce the heat to low and cook until the mixture is a deep golden brown color, 1 to 1½ hours longer. Add the sherry vinegar at the end to deglaze the pot. Let cool.

2. MAKE THE LIVERS: Toss the livers with the salt and caraway in a large bowl until coated. Place a cast-iron skillet over medium-high heat. When the skillet is very hot, add the livers and sear them on each side for 1 minute, then deglaze the pan with the sherry vinegar and cook until the liquid evaporates. Remove from the heat and let cool to room temperature.

3. MAKE THE MOUSSE: Combine the gribenes, chicken livers, caramelized onions, hard-boiled eggs, and stock in a blender. Blend until very smooth. Pass the mousse through a fine-mesh sieve into a medium bowl with a lid. Cover and refrigerate overnight. Taste and add salt if needed.

Yonak

HAIFA | Stepping back in time into this Romanian grill, founded in 1948, you're greeted with an array of Eastern European–style pickled tomatoes and cukes, a block of calf's foot jelly, schmaltzy chopped liver, ikra (fish roe dip), and roasted eggplant with garlic. This is followed by exemplary Romanian kebabs—perfect cylinders of beef and garlic, in equal amounts.

The scene at Maayan haBira.

Three Jews Walk into a Bar

Ever since God told Abraham to leave his father's house and travel to Canaan, the Jews have been a nomadic people. Even when they weren't in the midst of an outright exile (thanks, Babylonia) or fancy inquisition, Jews remained in a perpetual cycle of fleeing persecution and seeking economic opportunity elsewhere. There have been Jews living in the land of Israel continuously since Biblical times, but in the last few thousand years, they have spread to all four corners of the earth—even Antarctica.

This Diaspora is typically grouped into two broad categories: Sephardic Jews who lived on the Iberian Peninsula until the late fifteenth century, and Ashkenazi Jews who nominally grew out of a community that settled along the Rhine River during the Middle Ages.

But of course, it's all much more complicated. New research indicates that Ashkenazi Jews may be the descendants of Greeks and Persians who colonized northeastern Turkey two thousand years ago. Following the Spanish Inquisition, Sephardic Jews spread throughout the Ottoman Empire (Turkey, the Balkans, and the Levant) as well as North Africa (primarily Morocco and Algeria). Many stayed in Spain as conversos, covertly maintaining their faith. Some of these secret Jews accompanied Spanish and Portuguese settlers to the New World, establishing the oldest Jewish communities in the Americas.

And did we mention that there is a third group in the Diaspora? Mizrahi, or Eastern, Jews date their history back to antiquity in places like Babylonia (modern-day Iraq), Persia (Iran), and Yemen. Because Sephardic Jews often mixed with existing Mizrahi communities following their expulsion from Spain, Mizrahi Jews are often grouped together with Sephardic Jews, although their heritage is distinct.

Today, there are over 14 million Jews in the world. More than 80 percent live in Israel and the United States, in roughly equal numbers. But there are Jews in more than one hundred other countries—sometimes in minuscule communities—who will no doubt continue to adapt the local food customs of their host countries to the ever-evolving Jewish canon.

Pickled Green Tomatoes

Serves 4

Cut 4 medium green tomatoes into wedges and put them in a heatproof container. Combine 3 cups water, 1 cup white vinegar, ½ cup kosher salt, 1 teaspoon dill seed, 1 teaspoon whole allspice, 2 thinly sliced garlic cloves, and 1 cup dill sprigs in a medium saucepan. Bring to a boil, stirring to dissolve the salt, and pour over the tomatoes. Let cool to room temperature, then cover and refrigerate for at least 4 hours or overnight.

Quick Pickled Cucumbers

Serves 4

Whisk together 1 cup white vinegar, ½ cup sugar, and 2 tablespoons kosher salt in a small bowl. Cut 4 Kirby cucumbers crosswise into ¼-inch-thick slices. Sliver 2 shallots and a small handful of fresh mint leaves. Combine the cucumbers, shallots, mint, and a sprig of dill in a large bowl, then add the vinegar mixture. Cover and refrigerate for 48 hours.

Levinsky Market

TEL AVIV | Ronit Vered *(above)* with us at Mati, is one of Israel's most accomplished food journalists. Ronit examines the relationship between food and culture and explores the roots of the Jewish kitchen. Her writing shines a light on the local food artisans who are reviving and renewing the canon of Israeli cuisine.

Opposite: At Haim Rafael's specialty gourmet shop at 36 Levinsky, chefs and discerning eaters can buy hard-to-find products, like the elusive sheep's milk cheese from Israel's oldest dairy, Hameiri in Tzfat.

Rye Bread

Makes 1 loaf

3¾ cups bread flour

¾ cup rye flour

2 tablespoons sugar

½ teaspoon instant yeast

1½ cups warm water, plus more as needed

1 tablespoon caraway seeds

1 tablespoon plus 1 teaspoon kosher salt

1 tablespoon olive oil

Rye bread was virtually unknown to Sephardic and Mizrahi Jews, but it was a staple of the Ashkenazi diet in places like Russia and Poland. Considered inferior to wheat, rye grew well in the colder climate of Northern Europe, even under poor conditions (aka normal conditions for Jews). Ashkenazi Jews did bring rye bread to Israel, where it met an ignominious fate as government bread, the mass-produced, subsidized loaves that satisfied the basic requirement of being edible (I ate tons of it in Israeli boarding school). But it was in America that rye bread achieved its fame as the foundation upon which the Jewish deli sandwich was built.

Rye flour can be difficult to work with due to its low protein content, which means lower gluten formation and denser loaves. For sandwich rye, wheat is typically substituted for at least half of the flour. Our recipe is less than 20 percent rye flour—just enough so you know you're eating rye bread—but easy to work with and very forgiving. I used to think that the flavor of rye was the flavor of caraway seeds, but now I know that they are just really good friends. I am deeply suspicious of seedless rye.

We bake this bread every day at Abe Fisher to serve with our Montreal Smoked Short Ribs and Chicken Liver Mousse *(page 210)*. The leftovers are cut into croutons, fried, and tossed on salad, or turned into a cheesy bread pudding. But my favorite way to eat rye bread is to rip off a warm hunk and slather it with schmaltz, just like our ancestors did.

1. Mix together 1 cup of the bread flour, the rye flour, sugar, yeast, and water in a container with a lid. Cover and set aside in a warm place to rise for 30 minutes to 1 hour, or until doubled in volume.

2. Combine the remaining 2¾ cups bread flour, the caraway seeds, salt, and olive oil in a food processor. Add the risen dough on top and pulse, adding warm water a little at a time, just until the mixture comes together into a rough ball. (You won't need more than ⅓ cup water—overmixing makes denser bread.)

3. Scrape the dough into a lightly oiled bowl, cover loosely with plastic wrap, and let rise in a warm place for 30 minutes to 1 hour, or until doubled in volume. Punch it down, re-cover with plastic wrap, and let the dough rise again until it doubles.

4. Preheat the oven to 425°F. Transfer the dough to a baking sheet and shape a loaf roughly 10 by 4 inches. Let it rise for an hour in a warm place, covered, until almost doubled. Bake for 35 minutes, or until the internal temperature registers 190°F on an instant-read thermometer. Remove from the oven and let cool on a wire rack before slicing.

Pickled Mackerel

Serves 4

2 whole mackerel, cut into steaks

¼ cup plus 2 tablespoons kosher salt

6 cups water

2 cups distilled white vinegar

½ cup sugar

1 tablespoon whole allspice berries

1 tablespoon whole cardamom pods

1 tablespoon mustard seeds

1 tablespoon white peppercorns

1 lemon, sliced

Herring has played a critical role in European foodways for thousands of years, particularly in the lands surrounding the Baltic Sea. Each spring millions of the fish came to spawn in these brackish waters, where they were easily netted and consumed quickly due to their short shelf life. When the Dutch figured out how to preserve them with salt, herring became an important inland source of food as well. Jews living in Denmark, Germany, Poland, and Lithuania were actively involved in the herring trade, and the fish became a staple of their diet.

Salted herring only needed to be soaked to eat, but other methods were used to enhance the flavor of its dense, plush flesh, including this sweet-and-sour pickling technique. Here we apply the same treatment to mackerel, another oily fish that is inexpensive, easy to find, and produces a better yield than monkeying around with a barrel full of herring.

Serve with toasted Rye Bread *(opposite)* or Tam Tam crackers.

1. Place the mackerel steaks in a container with a lid. Dissolve 2 tablespoons of the salt in 4 cups of the water and pour over the fish. Cover and refrigerate overnight.

2. The next day, drain the fish and place in a container with a lid. Combine the vinegar, remaining ¼ cup salt, the sugar, allspice, cardamom, mustard seeds, peppercorns, and remaining 2 cups water in a medium saucepan. Bring to a boil, remove from the heat, and let cool to room temperature. Pour over the fish and lemon slices. Seal and let marinate in the refrigerator for at least 2 days. Refrigerated, the pickled fish will keep for up to 2 weeks.

Yehuda Sichel, Abe Fisher

PHILADELPHIA | Yehuda Sichel is the chef and our partner at Abe Fisher, the restaurant that explores the Ashkenazi traditions that inform much of the Jewish cooking in America. Yehuda, the grandson of Holocaust survivors, was raised in the Orthodox community in Baltimore. Like us, he felt his Jewish identity more strongly through food than in the yeshivas. In high school he was sent to a vocational boarding school, where he had his first experience with nonkosher food—a Whopper, which he scarfed down in an alley next to a dumpster.

The next nonkosher thing he ate was a second Whopper, immediately after the first. For work Yehuda loaded trucks and scraped plates for a catering company. He found satisfaction in the rare moments when he was given the chance to cook. Then he got hired at a kosher deli where he made sandwiches for the next three years.

Culinary school in Jerusalem confirmed his desire to pursue a career in the kitchen. Shortly after Yehuda returned to the U.S., we hired him as a line cook at Zahav, which had recently opened and was still struggling to find its footing. He was quickly promoted to sous chef. When we decided to open Abe Fisher, Yehuda was the only chef we needed to talk to. He has spent the last several years carving out a living, breathing vision of Jewish-American food that venerates tradition while incorporating the diversity that makes Philadelphia one of the most exciting food scenes in the country.

In addition to his duties at Abe Fisher, Yehuda is our resident expert on Philadelphia's Chinatown restaurants and an inaugural participant in Zahav's annual Jewish Christmas, where we honor the important Jewish-American Yuletide ritual of eating Chinese food and watching movies.

Above from left: Abe Fisher's signature dish, Montreal Style–Smoked Short Ribs; Yehuda; and the lively scene at Abe Fisher.

This is pure Abe Fisher—not your grandma's: borscht tartare, hard-boiled egg topped with smoked trout roe, and homemade ranch potato chips.

Cured Trout

Makes 4 fillets

¼ cup gin

1 cup kosher salt

2 tablespoons sugar

Rind of 1 lemon, chopped

½ cup chopped fresh dill

2 whole skin-on rainbow trout, butterflied, pin bones removed

Smoked or cured fish has always played an important role in the Jewish diet. Because it is pareve (neither meat nor dairy) and does not require cooking, it is a versatile addition to the kosher household and can be eaten with any meal and on Shabbat.

Curing fish at home is incredibly easy and a lot cheaper than buying it at a fancy store. We use trout because it is readily available and inexpensive. In addition, its thin fillets require less curing time and thus deliver quicker gratification. Feel free to substitute salmon and adjust the curing time based on the thickness of the fish.

Mix together the gin, salt, sugar, lemon rind, and dill in a small bowl. Rub this mixture all over the trout fillets. Place them in a baking dish, cover, and refrigerate for 12 hours. When you're ready to serve the fish, rinse it under cool running water, then pat it dry with paper towels. Peel away the skin and slice the fish very thinly on the bias. Watch for stray pin bones, and serve with fresh Rye Bread (page 218) and butter or cream cheese.

Smoked Whitefish Dip

Serves 4

1½ to 2 pounds whole smoked whitefish

½ cup mayonnaise

⅓ cup chopped celery

⅓ cup finely chopped red onion

¼ cup chopped fresh dill

¼ cup chopped fresh parsley

Fresh lemon juice

Kosher salt

This super-simple and utterly delicious dish is prepared from store-bought smoked fish. Whitefish is a catchall term for a number of freshwater species that were an important food source for landlocked European Jews. Along with pike and carp, whitefish is the third traditional component of gefilte fish. Whitefish turns a gorgeous golden color when smoked, a traditional preservation method before the advent of refrigeration. When Ashkenazi Jews arrived in America, they found that the Great Lakes offered a very similar species of whitefish, and an appetizing-store classic was born.

Serve with toasted Rye Bread *(page 218)* or Tam Tam crackers.

Remove the skin and discard. Flake the fish with a fork into big chunks and transfer to a large bowl. Gently fold in the mayonnaise, celery, onion, dill, and parsley. Taste and add lemon juice and salt as needed.

CHAPTER 11

Soups,
Stews,
Stuffed

"Next to the definition of comfort food in any dictionary, there ought to be a picture of Azura."

In a small square near the main thoroughfare of Jerusalem's Machane Yehuda Market sits a restaurant called **Azura**. The courtyard is filled with café tables and sheltering umbrellas. In the coffee shop next door, old men smoke, play cards, and argue about politics. A woman across the way, seated at a table, calmly forms kubbe dumplings by hand, pinching off a piece of semolina dough and, with her thumb, making an indentation for the stuffing of meat, onions, and spices. By the time they are sealed shut, the kubbe are magically all the same size. These dumplings are part of the kibbe universe, popular throughout the Levant—a collection of fried, baked, and raw dishes related by their use of bulgur, semolina, or even ground rice.

You can tell you're near Azura by the smell of kerosene burning. Just inside the restaurant, a counter separates the kitchen from the small dining room. A dozen cauldrons gently simmer away over the burners. Azura serves four kinds of kubbe soup; hearty stews like the Sephardic classic beef sofrito; moussaka; meatballs in tomato sauce; eggplant stuffed with lamb and pine nuts; and all the stuffed and braised vegetables you can imagine, from vine leaves to whole onions to cabbage.

שׁ... הַ... גַג... בֹּ... הַ...

גַּגּוֹצִים רַבִּים שֶׁחִפְּשׂוּ קְצָת חַב

עַל אֵשׁ קְטַנָּה

וְכָל רֵיחוֹת תַּפּוּחֵי הָאֲדָמָה הָאוֹרֶז

וְקִצּוּצוֹת הַבָּשָׂר שֶׁחָדְרוּ לַנְּחִירֵי

רַ... לָרֶגַע אֶת אִמִּי

אֲנִי בָּא וְאֵלֶיהָ לֹא

לָלֶכֶת...

יוֹסִי בָּנָאִי

מִתּוֹךְ: כְּשֶׁאִמָּא שֶׁלִּי הִ״תָה מִ

1996

Previous spread: At Azura in Jerusalem's Machane Yehuda Market, a woman makes kubbe dumplings. *This page:* a table at Azura is laid with time-honored soups and stews.

Azura

JERUSALEM | Azura has practiced slow food long before there was such a movement, though the restaurant surely qualifies for membership. "The Azura family is the main supporter of kerosene cookers in Israel," says the Jerusalem-based culinary reporter and restaurant critic Amit Aaronsohn with a smile. "Just the smell of those pots is instant nostalgia. It's the way my grandmother cooked."

Four sons and one daughter *(above)* of Ezra Sherfler, the original Kurdish owner, still run the institution began by their father seventy years ago.

The surface of each pot is slicked with grease and stained by spices in shades of red, orange, and yellow.

Azura's founder, Ezra Sherfler, was fourteen when he started washing dishes at a nearby Turkish restaurant. He learned to cook by watching the chef. Ezra ran Azura for sixty years; now it is run by several of his nine children, including that dumpling-making daughter.

When Azura opened in 1952, cooking with kerosene was a necessity in the new economically challenged country. For Israelis who lived through those lean years, the smell of kerosene provokes nostalgia for that transformational time. For younger Israelis it recalls memories of their grandmothers' cooking. Comfort food is, by definition, a link to a time or place when we felt at ease, free of the anxiety of everyday life. And there is something about the soups and stews, the dumplings, and the stuffed vegetables at Azura that warms the soul as well as the body.

Taste memories can be a powerful emotional connection to bygone times. And they can satisfy a longing for a past to which we cannot return. The late, great actor and musician Yossi Banai grew up near Machane Yehuda. A poem he wrote hangs on the wall outside the restaurant:

At the restaurant of Azura
In the small market behind the
large market
I saw in the kitchen, in pots over
kerosene flames
Many longings looking for some
warmth over a small fire
And all the smells of potatoes, rice
And spinach patties
That permeated my nostrils
Brought back, for a moment,
My mother . . .

Chamo Kubbe

Serves 4

KUBBE

- 1 (3- to 4-pound) chicken
- 1 tablespoon plus a pinch of kosher salt
- 2 teaspoons plus a pinch of Hawaij Spice Blend (page 150)
- 2 medium carrots, peeled and coarsely chopped
- 1 onion, chopped
- 1 garlic head, halved horizontally
- 1 (2-inch) piece fresh turmeric, peeled and chopped, or 2 teaspoons ground turmeric
- 2⅓ cups water
- ⅔ cup bulgur
- 1 cup semolina flour

SOUP

- 2 tablespoons canola oil
- 3 medium carrots, peeled and sliced
- 1 onion, chopped
- 4 garlic cloves, thinly sliced
- 1 tablespoon kosher salt
- 1 teaspoon Hawaij Spice Blend (page 150)
- 1 (15-ounce) can chickpeas, drained and rinsed
- 1 yellow squash, chopped

Kubbe is a soft semolina dumpling served in soup. There are nearly as many versions of kubbe as there are Iraqi and Kurdish grandmothers, and the soups range from *hamusta* ("sour"), a light broth containing celery, chard, and summer squash, perked up with a healthy dose of fresh lemon juice, to *adom* ("red"), a heartier version flavored with beets. Chamo kubbe turns yellow with the addition of turmeric and is thickened with chickpeas.

Kubbe are typically stuffed with a ground beef mixture. In this recipe, however, we use a whole chicken to make the soup broth, reserving the meat as the basis for the filling. These dumplings are a labor of love, but that's a big part of what makes them taste so good.

1. MAKE THE KUBBE: Remove the legs, breasts, and thighs from the chicken and reserve the carcass. Rub the chicken pieces with 1 tablespoon of the salt and 2 teaspoons of the hawaij, place in a container, cover, and refrigerate overnight.

2. The next day, put the carrots, onion, garlic, turmeric, chicken pieces, and carcass in a large pot and add enough water to just cover the chicken. Bring to a boil over medium-high heat, then reduce the heat to medium-low and simmer, uncovered, for 45 minutes. Remove the breasts, legs, and thighs and set aside; leave the carcass in the pot. Simmer for 2 to 3 more hours, or until the stock is flavorful and a rich golden color.

3. When the chicken pieces are cool enough to handle, discard the skin. Pick the meat from the bones and finely chop. Taste and add a pinch each of salt and hawaij. This is the filling.

4. Bring 1⅓ cups of the water to a boil in a small pot. Put the bulgur in a heatproof bowl. Pour the boiling water over the bulgur, cover, and let stand until the liquid is absorbed, about 20 to 25 minutes.

5. Mix the cooked bulgur, the semolina, and the remaining 1 cup water in a bowl until it comes together into a dough. If it's too sticky, add a little more semolina; if it's too dry, add a few more drops of water. Cover and refrigerate for at least 30 minutes or up to 4 hours. Turn the dough onto a lightly floured surface and divide it into 8 pieces. Using your hands, pat each piece into a thin, 6-inch-long oval shape. Place a couple of spoonfuls of filling in the middle of each one, fold the dough over the filling, and press the edges to seal the dumpling.

6. Strain the stock into a clean pot and discard the chicken carcass and vegetables. Bring to a boil over medium-high heat. Add the kubbe, one at a time, bringing the stock back to a boil each time. Cover and cook for 25 minutes over medium heat (the stock should be gently bubbling the whole time).

7. MEANWHILE, MAKE THE SOUP: Heat the oil in a clean pot. Add the carrots, onion, garlic, salt, and hawaij and cook for 5 minutes, or until the vegetables are soft. Add the chickpeas, kubbe, all of the stock, and the yellow squash. Cook for 15 minutes, or until the squash is tender. Taste and add salt if needed.

Opera Bean Soup

Serves 4 to 6

2 tablespoons canola oil

1 onion, chopped

5 garlic cloves, thinly sliced

1 pound dried navy beans, soaked in water overnight and drained

2 serrano chiles, punctured and left whole

1 tablespoon smoked paprika

4 cups tomato juice

4 cups water, plus more as needed

1 teaspoon kosher salt

Lemon juice

Handful of chopped cilantro

I cherish **Opera** restaurant first and foremost for its unrivaled Yemenite soup. Three varieties compete for my attention whenever I can make it to Hadera, an hour north of Tel Aviv. But this simple bean soup, fortified with earthy, smoky paprika and a touch of heat, is a reminder of how the combination of humble ingredients and honest cooking can produce something that is absolutely stunning.

Heat the oil in a deep pot over medium-high heat. Add the onion and garlic and cook until translucent, about 5 minutes. Add the beans, chiles, paprika, tomato juice, and water. Bring to a simmer and cook for 2 hours. Add the salt, then cook for another 2 hours, adding more water as needed to keep the beans submerged, until they are tender and creamy. Remove the chiles before serving. Taste and add a squeeze of lemon juice and salt. Scatter cilantro over each bowl and serve.

Opera

HADERA | Rachel Arcovi *(right)* and her restaurant have meant a lot to me. I met my half-sister, Meirav, for the first time at Opera, and I loved it so much that I brought my brother, Dave, back for what would turn out to be one of our last meals together.

At the end of that meal, I asked Rachel in broken Hebrew what spices she used in her Yemenite soup, and she kindly sent me home with a container of cumin, turmeric, and black pepper. I use that combination to this day, but I've still never been able to make soup as good as hers.

Yemenite-Style Veal Osso Buco
with Yellow Rice

Serves 4

4 veal shanks

2 tablespoons plus 1 teaspoon kosher salt

2 tablespoons Hawaij Spice Blend *(page 150)*

1 tablespoon canola oil

1 onion, chopped

Garlic cloves from 1 head, chopped

3 carrots, peeled and chopped

2 tablespoons tomato paste

4 medium Yukon Gold potatoes, quartered

6 cups chicken stock

Yellow Rice, for serving

Calf's foot was the original cheap cut used to flavor Yemenite soup. In these more prosperous times, chicken and beef have largely taken over the Yemenite soup game. But there's no substitute for the lip-smacking qualities that veal brings to the table. Here we braise veal shanks with hawaij to fall-apart tenderness. Served with yellow rice flavored with more hawaij, this is a great stand-in for the classic Italian combination of osso buco and risotto Milanese at your next dinner party.

1. Rub the veal shanks with 2 tablespoons of the salt and the hawaij. Cover and refrigerate for 48 hours.

2. Preheat the oven to 275°F. Heat the oil in a deep ovenproof pot (big enough to hold all the shanks) over medium-high heat. Sear the veal shanks on all sides and transfer to a plate. Reduce the heat to medium-low and add the onion and garlic. Cook until the onion is soft, about 5 minutes, then add the remaining 1 teaspoon salt and the carrots.

3. Cook for 2 to 3 minutes, or just until the carrots begin to soften. Stir in the tomato paste and cook for 30 seconds. Add the potatoes and veal shanks to the pot. Pour in the chicken stock. Cover and transfer to the oven. Braise until the veal is fork-tender, about 3 hours. Serve with the Yellow Rice.

Yellow Rice

Makes 6 cups

2 tablespoons olive oil

2 cups jasmine rice

1 tablespoon kosher salt

1 tablespoon Hawaij Spice Blend *(page 150)*

4 cups water

1. Preheat the oven to 350°F. Heat the oil in a medium skillet, add the rice, salt, and hawaij, and toast for a few minutes, or until fragrant. Transfer the mixture to a baking dish (or a deep saucepan with a lid) and add the water. Cover tightly with foil. Bake for 25 minutes, or until the rice is tender and the liquid has been absorbed.

2. Remove from the oven and let sit, covered, for at least 10 minutes; the texture will improve the longer it rests. Uncover, fluff with a fork, and serve.

Lamb Shank Siniya

Serves 4

4 lamb shanks

2 tablespoons plus a pinch of kosher salt

1 tablespoon plus 1 teaspoon ground coriander

1 tablespoon crushed Aleppo pepper

2 teaspoons ground caraway

2 tablespoons canola oil

1 onion, chopped

4 garlic cloves, chopped

1 yellow bell pepper, chopped

1 red bell pepper, chopped

1 Fresno or other red chile, punctured and left whole

¼ cup tomato paste

1 tablespoon smoked paprika

1 cup cilantro sprigs

6 cups chicken stock

⅓ cup Quick Tehina Sauce
(page 145)

3 tablespoons ground sumac

Tomato Bulgur
(opposite), **for serving**

Siniya is a classic Arabic dish enjoyed by the Lebanese, Syrians, Druze, and especially Palestinians. Not unlike a Middle Eastern shepherd's pie, the dish features ground meat, typically lamb, mixed with aromatics, spices, and herbs and baked under a crust of tehina and pine nuts. In this version, we swap in braised lamb shanks for the ground lamb. Then, right before serving, we top the shanks with tehina sauce and put them under the broiler for a few minutes to glaze them.

Serve with Tomato Bulgur (opposite).

1. Rub the shanks with 2 tablespoons of the salt, the coriander, Aleppo pepper, and caraway. Cover and refrigerate overnight.

2. The next day, preheat the broiler. Place the shanks on a baking sheet or in a cast-iron skillet and broil for 8 to 10 minutes, turning once, to brown the lamb on both sides. Reduce the oven temperature to 275°F.

3. Heat the oil in a deep ovenproof pot over medium-high heat. Add the onion, garlic, and a big pinch of salt and cook until the onion is soft, about 5 minutes. Add the bell peppers and chile. When they have softened, stir in the tomato paste, paprika, and cilantro. Nestle the shanks into the vegetable mixture and pour in the stock. Cover and transfer to the oven. Braise for 4 hours, or until the meat is tender and separates easily from the bone. Remove from the oven and turn on the broiler.

4. Transfer the shanks to a large cast-iron skillet (you may need to do this in batches). Spoon some of the juices from the pot into the skillet. Drizzle the tehina sauce on top of the shanks and broil for 3 to 4 minutes, or until they are glossy and the tehina looks like melted cheese. Sprinkle with the sumac and serve with the Tomato Bulgur.

Tomato Bulgur

Serves 4

4 cups tomato juice

2 teaspoons kosher salt

1 teaspoon smoked paprika

2 cups bulgur

Bulgur is one of the world's oldest processed foods. It is mentioned in the Bible and was appreciated by ancient cultures as far-flung as the Babylonians, the Chinese, and the Romans.

Bulgur is made by boiling whole kernels of wheat, drying them in the sun, and coarsely cracking the hardened kernels. The resulting product is mold- and insect-resistant, with a long shelf life and excellent nutritional properties—all useful traits for ensuring a reliable food supply in early civilization. In addition, because it's already cooked, bulgur can be prepared quickly. By rehydrating bulgur in a flavorful liquid (here we use tomato juice), we add another dimension to a versatile ingredient that can be used in soups and salads, as a stuffing or a side dish in place of rice or couscous, or to make kibbe.

Combine the tomato juice, salt, and paprika in a medium saucepan and bring to a boil. Put the bulgur in a heatproof bowl. Pour the boiling tomato juice mixture over the bulgur, cover, and let stand until the liquid is absorbed, 20 to 25 minutes.

Andrew Henshaw, Zahav

PHILADELPHIA | When Andrew started as a line cook at Zahav, his previous experience was working in corporate dining in the suburbs. In a few short years, he worked his way up the ranks to become executive sous chef, keeping a brigade of more than a dozen cooks humming. Andrew exemplifies the "first in, last out" work ethic that is the cornerstone of any successful kitchen career. He's also one of the few people who can deal with my neuroses. And, oh yes, he helped Steve and me prepare every recipe in this book from scratch to photograph. Even though he did make the couscous, he confided that he'd probably use store-bought!

Couscous

Makes 2 to 3 cups

1½ cups fine semolina

About 2 teaspoons kosher salt

2 cinnamon sticks

Lemon juice

2 tablespoons olive oil

Many people assume that couscous, the staple North African dish, is a grain. In fact it is a tiny pasta or dumpling made from semolina flour and water that has been rolled between the hands to form tiny pellets. These pellets are then traditionally steamed in a couscoussière over a simmering stew so that the couscous absorbs the flavorful vapors.

Steamed couscous can be dried and later rehydrated with boiling water. Sure, you can buy instant couscous that has been treated in this manner. It is certainly convenient, but we don't think it compares to properly prepared fresh couscous, which is fluffy and ethereal and worth every minute of your labor. But don't take our word for it; try it yourself at least once.

1. Fill a small spray bottle or bowl with ¼ cup water. Combine the semolina and salt in a large bowl. Sprinkle the mixture a few times with water and mix with your fingertips until damp. Keep sprinkling and mixing until the mixture looks grainy but doesn't clump together. Rub the couscous between your hands until it forms crumbs. Transfer to a fine-mesh sieve or small-holed colander set over another large bowl. Push the grains through with your fingers into the bowl and discard the leftover clumps.

2. Pour a few inches of water into a large pot and add the cinnamon sticks. Line a steamer basket or metal sieve with cheesecloth, a large coffee filter, or a layer of paper towels. Bring the water to a boil. Pour the sifted semolina mixture into the prepared steamer basket and set over the boiling water. Cover and steam for 1 hour, or until soft and fluffy. Remove from the heat. Pour the steamed couscous into a bowl, fluff with a fork, and push through the sieve one more time, discarding the clumps. Add more water to the pot as needed and bring to a boil. Return the couscous to the lined steamer basket and steam, covered, for 1 more hour. Fluff and toss with some lemon juice, more salt, and the olive oil.

In the ancient city of Tzfat, Zahava Lagziel *(page 286)* makes fresh couscous daily.

Vegetable Tagine

Serves 4

2 tablespoons
canola oil

1 onion, chopped,
plus 4 small
onions, peeled
and halved

4 garlic cloves,
thinly sliced

1 tablespoon
kosher salt

1 teaspoon Hawaij
Spice Blend
(page 150)

1 head cauliflower,
cut into florets

2 medium carrots,
peeled and cut
into chunks

2 quarts vegetable
stock

Couscous
(page 241), **for
serving**

A tagine is a North African stew named for the vessel in which it is cooked. The conical-shaped lid is designed to capture steam and return it to the circular base where the stew is cooking. This minimizes the amount of liquid required for cooking—a practical benefit in areas with limited water supplies—and concentrates the flavors.

But you don't really need a tagine to cook a tagine. This recipe for a quick and simple vegetable stew is designed to highlight fresh couscous. Feel free to substitute other vegetables and spice blends as your pantry and preferences dictate.

1. Heat the oil in a large saucepan over medium-high heat. Add the chopped onion, garlic, salt, and hawaij and cook, stirring, for 5 minutes, or until the onion is translucent. Add the remaining vegetables and cook for 2 minutes, then add the stock. Bring to a boil, cover, and reduce the heat to medium-low.

2. Cook until the vegetables are softened, 15 to 20 minutes. Remove from the heat. Taste and add salt as needed. Serve with the Couscous.

Guetta

TEL AVIV | When his European restaurant did not succeed, Rafi Guetta did what everyone should do: He listened to his mother! Leah advised him to cook the Tripolitan food of their Libyan forebears, so Rafi reopened, and the rest is history.

A meal at Guetta is a delicious reminder of the diversity of Israeli cuisine. The chiles and spices of North Africa combine with Libya's colonial Italian influence to produce unique dishes. Highlights of our nap-inducing lunch included chirshi, the sweet-and-sour pumpkin-based condiment (we make it with squash, *page 196*); rib-sticking stuffed vegetables; fish cakes in a peppery tomato sauce; the exquisite fluffy couscous shown here; and mafroum: potatoes that are stuffed, fried, and braised (*page 255*).

Beef Tongue with Beans
Serves 6

BRINE

- 1 cup kosher salt
- ½ cup sugar
- 2 tablespoons ground allspice
- 2 tablespoons freshly ground black pepper
- 1 tablespoon fennel seeds
- 1 quart water
- 1 quart ice water
- 1 (3-pound) beef tongue, pierced all over with a fork

BRAISE

- 2 tablespoons canola oil
- 1 large onion, chopped
- 2 garlic cloves, chopped
- 2 celery ribs, chopped
- 1 carrot, peeled and chopped
- Kosher salt
- 1 quart chicken stock
- 1 cup dried large white beans

FRIED ONIONS

- ¼ cup canola oil
- 3 onions, thinly sliced
- 2 teaspoons kosher salt

Fresh parsley, chopped, for topping

Our dinner at **Maayan haBira** in Haifa starts with a salatim spread heavy on Ashkenazi influence. As a solo classical violinist gives way to a Bob Marley cover band, it is time for the meat, and our table nearly buckles under the weight of it. There is smoked goose leg, garlicky veal-and-lamb sausage, veal spare ribs, and smoked beef shoulder. And last but not least: a platter of pillow-soft braised beef tongue on a bed of tender and creamy beans, topped with crispy fried onions.

1. BRINE THE TONGUE: Combine the salt, sugar, allspice, pepper, fennel seeds, and water in a medium pot. Bring to a boil, stirring to dissolve the salt and sugar, then remove from the heat, add the ice water, and let cool to room temperature.

2. Pour the cooled brine into a covered container that is large enough to fit the tongue and brine. Submerge the tongue in the brine, cover, and refrigerate for at least 10 days or up to 2 weeks.

3. BRAISE THE TONGUE: Preheat the oven to 275°F. Heat the oil in a deep ovenproof pot over medium-high heat. Add the onion, garlic, celery, carrot, and a pinch of salt. Cook until the vegetables begin to soften, 5 to 7 minutes. Remove the tongue from the brine, pat dry, and transfer to the pot. Add the chicken stock and some water if necessary to completely submerge the tongue. Cover and braise in the oven for 2 hours. Add the dried beans to the pot, making sure they're

submerged in the liquid, then braise for another 2 hours, or until the tongue is easily pierced with a fork and the beans are tender.

4. MEANWHILE, MAKE THE FRIED ONIONS: Heat the oil in a cast-iron skillet and add the onions and salt. Cook over medium-low heat until the onions are deep golden brown and crispy, about 1 hour. Drain on paper towels.

5. Transfer the tongue to a cutting board. Peel and discard the outer membrane from the tongue (it should pull off easily) and cut into thick slices. Drain almost all the liquid from the pot (reserve for soup!). Serve the tongue with the beans, topped with the fried onions and fresh parsley.

Gohar

KFAR SABA | It's almost inconceivable that a restaurant this authentic could exist in a suburban shopping strip. Gohar's Persian-inspired richly flavored simmering stews and succulent stuffed vegetables are worthy of adoring crowds. *Opposite:* A Persian rice timbale with peas, greens, and crispy potatoes.

Brisket Stewed with Black-Eyed Peas

Serves 8 to 10

1 (6-pound) beef brisket

1½ tablespoons kosher salt

1 tablespoon ground turmeric

1 dried lime, crushed and ground in a spice grinder

¼ cup canola oil

3 large onions, finely chopped

Garlic cloves from 1 head, thinly sliced

2 quarts chicken stock

2 cups dried black-eyed peas, soaked for 4 hours or up to overnight

3 bunches lacinato kale (about 15 stalks), stemmed and chopped

Handful chopped fresh dill

We ate this soupy-stew at **Gohar**, a Persian restaurant at the end of a strip mall in the industrial area of Kfar Saba, north of Tel Aviv. A recent tech boom in the neighborhood has made parking difficult, but the pots of stick-to-your-ribs Persian classics set on a hot plate for the lunch rush remain unchanged. The richness of the brisket (we like the flat, or first-cut) and black-eyed peas is perfectly balanced by the stewed greens, the haunting acidity of dried lime, and tons of fresh dill.

1. Rub the brisket with the salt, turmeric, and dried lime. Cover and refrigerate for at least 24 hours or up to 2 days.

2. Preheat the oven to 500°F. Place the brisket on a rack in a baking pan. Roast for 20 minutes. Remove from the oven and set aside. Reduce the oven temperature to 275°F.

3. Heat the oil in a deep ovenproof pot. Add the onions and garlic and cook, stirring, until the onions are translucent. Add the brisket and the stock. Cover and braise in the oven for 2 hours. Check and add water if necessary. Remove from the oven, add the black-eyed peas and kale, cover, and braise for 2 more hours, or until the beans and brisket are fork-tender. Serve with the dill.

Persian Meatballs with Beet Sauce

Serves 4

MEATBALLS

- 1 pound ground beef
- ½ cup chopped fresh parsley
- ½ onion, grated
- 2 tablespoons seltzer
- 2 teaspoons ground cumin
- 1½ teaspoons kosher salt
- 1 teaspoon smoked paprika
- 1 teaspoon freshly ground black pepper
- ¼ cup canola oil

BEET SAUCE

- 1 onion, finely chopped
- 2 garlic cloves, thinly sliced
- 2 tablespoons tamarind paste
- 2 tablespoons pomegranate molasses
- 2 large red beets, peeled and finely chopped
- 1 quart chicken stock
- Fresh mint leaves

Tamarind and pomegranate molasses in the unexpected beet sauce contribute this classic Persian sweet-and-sour flavor profile to these otherwise straightforward meatballs. Serve over Yellow Rice *(page 237)* for a color explosion.

1. MAKE THE MEATBALLS: Preheat the oven to 275°F. Mix together the ground beef, parsley, onion, seltzer, cumin, salt, paprika, and pepper in a medium bowl. Shape the mixture into golf ball–size meatballs. Heat the oil in a deep ovenproof pot over medium-high heat. Sear the meatballs on all sides, about 6 minutes, then transfer to a plate. Do not wipe out the pot.

2. MAKE THE SAUCE: Add the onion and garlic to the pot and cook over medium-high heat until the onions are soft and translucent, about 5 minutes. Stir in the tamarind paste and pomegranate molasses and cook, stirring, for 1 to 2 minutes. Add the beets, meatballs, and stock. Cover and braise in the oven for 45 minutes, or until the meatballs are cooked through and the beets are tender.

3. Remove from the oven and transfer the meatballs to a plate. Place the pot over medium-high heat, bring to a boil, and cook until the sauce has reduced by half, about 15 minutes. Taste and add salt as needed. Return the meatballs to the pot, toss to coat with the sauce, and warm through. Scatter on mint leaves before serving.

A. This is high-end food play: Flatten a grape leaf and spoon the filling evenly on the bottom third.

B. Fold the bottom of the leaf over the filling, tuck in the sides, and roll tightly like a burrito.

Stuffed Grape Leaves
with Pomegranate Molasses

Makes about 25

⅓ cup jasmine rice, soaked in water for 4 hours at room temperature or refrigerated overnight

1 pound ground beef

¼ cup Spicy Tomato Sauce or other good tomato sauce

1 cup chopped fresh parsley

1 large egg

2 teaspoons kosher salt

1 teaspoon freshly ground black pepper

1 teaspoon paprika

25 grape leaves (from a 16-ounce jar)

1 carrot, peeled and sliced

1 onion, finely chopped

½ cup pomegranate juice

¼ cup date molasses

1 cup water

We savored these simple grape leaves stuffed with rice and beef at **Gohar**, the Persian restaurant in Kfar Saba, north of Tel Aviv. Iran produces an enormous amount of fruit, which appears in a wide range of traditional Persian dishes in both its fresh and preserved forms. The addition of pomegranate juice and date molasses to the braising liquid is what makes the flavor of these grape leaves special.

1. Preheat the oven to 375°F. Drain the rice and place it in a large bowl along with the beef, tomato sauce, parsley, egg, salt, pepper, and paprika. Mix well.

2. Bring a large pot of water to a boil. Fill a bowl with ice water. Blanch the grape leaves, a few at a time, in the boiling water for 3 minutes then transfer to the ice bath to stop the cooking. Remove the leaves from the water and place them in a single layer on parchment paper.

3. Spoon 1 to 2 tablespoons of the filling onto the bottom third of each grape leaf and roll it up: Fold the bottom of the leaf over the filling, tuck in the sides, and roll tightly like a burrito.

4. Arrange the carrot and onion in the bottom of an ovenproof pot. Place the stuffed grape leaves on top in a single layer. Add the pomegranate juice, date molasses, and water. Cover the pot and bake for 25 minutes. Remove from the oven and let steam, covered, for 6 minutes. The leaves will get nice and glossy. Uncover and place the pot over medium-high heat. Cook until the sauce has reduced by half, about 10 minutes, gently stirring the grape leaves every few minutes to keep them from burning. Serve the stuffed grape leaves drizzled with the pomegranate sauce from the pot.

Tomato Sauce

Makes about 1½ cups

1 tablespoon olive oil

1 onion, finely chopped

3 garlic cloves, thinly sliced

½ teaspoon kosher salt

1 (15-ounce) can crushed tomatoes

Heat the oil in a medium saucepan over medium-high heat. Add the onion, garlic, and salt and cook until the onion is translucent, then add the tomatoes. Reduce the heat to medium-low and cook, stirring, for 10 to 15 minutes. If you like your sauce extra smooth, let it cool slightly, then puree in a blender or food processor.

SPICY TOMATO SAUCE: Add 1 tablespoon crushed Aleppo pepper to the onion in the pan. Toast for a minute, then add the tomatoes and cook as directed.

Chicken Wrapped in Chard

Makes 6

6 large Swiss chard leaves with stems

6 skin-on, boneless chicken thighs

3 tablespoons canola oil

1 onion, minced

3 garlic cloves, thinly sliced

Kosher salt

6 cinnamon sticks

1 cup sour cherry juice

2 tablespoons pomegranate molasses

This is a festive Persian treatment for chicken thighs, which remain tender and juicy even when long-cooked. Sour cherry juice and pomegranate molasses are the perfect foil for the rich dark-meat chicken. Just don't eat the cinnamon sticks!

1. Preheat the oven to 400°F. Bring a pot of water to a boil. Fill a bowl with ice water. Fold each chard leaf in half and cut the rib from the stem, reserving the leaves. Blanch the chard leaves in the boiling water, a few at a time, for 30 seconds, then use tongs to transfer them to the ice bath and quickly remove. Drain on paper towels and set aside.

2. Remove the skin from the chicken thighs and place on a cutting board along with the chard stems. With a very sharp knife, chop the chicken skins and chard stems together until minced. Heat the oil in a medium skillet over medium-high heat. Add the onion, garlic, chard–chicken skin mixture, and a big pinch of salt and sauté until soft, about 10 minutes. Remove from the heat.

3. Pound the chicken thighs to a ¼-inch thickness and sprinkle with salt. Place a blanched chard leaf on the cutting board. Lay the chicken on top, spoon a few tablespoons of the filling in the center, then add the cinnamon stick and roll up like a burrito.

4. Arrange the wrapped chicken rolls in a single layer in an ovenproof pot. Add the cherry juice, drizzle with the pomegranate molasses, cover, and transfer to the oven. Braise for 20 to 25 minutes, or until cooked through. Remove from the oven and transfer the chicken to a plate. Place the pot over medium-high heat and cook until the sauce has reduced by half, about 6 minutes. Serve the chicken drizzled with the sauce.

A. Lay a blanched chard leaf on a board, top with a pounded chicken thigh, and spoon on the filling.

B. Add a cinnamon stick and roll the chard and chicken around the stuffing like a burrito.

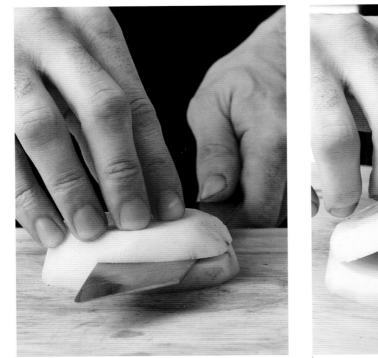

A. Make a horizontal cut almost through each potato half, making sure it is still intact.

B. Stuff each cut potato half with a few tablespoons of beef filling.

C. Ready a bowl of beaten eggs and one of matzo meal. Dunk each potato in the matzo, then the egg.

D. Roll the stuffed potato again in the matzo meal to cover all sides.

Mafroum
Libyan Stuffed Potatoes
Makes 8

- 1 pound ground beef
- 1 cup chopped fresh parsley
- 1 onion, grated
- 2 garlic cloves, minced
- 2 teaspoons smoked paprika
- 1 teaspoon ground cumin
- 1 teaspoon ground coriander
- 1 teaspoon ground caraway
- 1 teaspoon kosher salt
- 4 large Yukon Gold potatoes
- 2 large eggs
- 1½ cups matzo meal
- ¼ cup canola oil, plus more as needed
- 1½ cups Tomato Sauce *(page 251)* or other good tomato sauce

This dish proves the notion that Jews have never met a vegetable they didn't try to stuff. Mafroum was part of an eye-opening lunch in Tel Aviv at **Guetta**, Rafi Guetta's ode to his mother's Tripolitan cooking (that's the food of Tripoli in Libya). Planks of potatoes are improbably sliced open lengthwise, leaving one end attached. The potatoes are then stuffed, battered, pan-fried, and (finally) braised in a tomato sauce spiked with cumin, coriander, and caraway, the holy trinity of spices in North African Jewish cooking.

1. Mix the beef, parsley, onion, garlic, spices, and salt in a medium bowl.

2. Peel the potatoes, square off the tops and bottoms, and cut each in half horizontally. Make a horizontal cut about 90 percent of the way through each potato piece. Beat the eggs in a shallow bowl for the egg wash. Put the matzo meal in another shallow bowl.

3. Stuff each potato piece with a few tablespoons of the beef filling. Press the potato into the matzo meal on all sides, coat it with the egg wash, then dip it in the matzo meal again to recoat on all sides.

4. Preheat the oven to 350°F. Heat the oil in an ovenproof pot over medium-high heat. Working in batches and adding more oil as needed, brown the stuffed potatoes on all sides. Transfer the potatoes to a plate and wipe out the pot. Pour the tomato sauce into the pot, arrange the potatoes on top in a single layer, cover, and bake until the stuffing is cooked through and the potatoes are tender, about 45 minutes.

Stuffed Eggplant

Serves 4

2 large eggplants, halved lengthwise

2 teaspoons kosher salt

FILLING

1 pound ground lamb

1½ onions, ½ grated and 1 finely chopped

4 garlic cloves, 2 grated and 2 finely minced

¼ cup mixed chopped fresh cilantro and parsley

2 teaspoons plus a pinch of kosher salt

1 tablespoon Merguez Spice Blend *(page 151)*

1 tablespoon canola oil

1 red bell pepper, finely chopped

1 yellow bell pepper, finely chopped

2 tablespoons tomato paste

½ cup crushed tomatoes

¼ cup pine nuts

1 cup Tomato Sauce *(page 251)* or other good tomato sauce

This utterly delicious dish delivers a big visual bang on the plate. It would be at home on any table in Israel. Try this recipe in summer when local heirloom eggplants are at their sweetest.

1. Preheat the oven to 400°F. Score the cut sides of the eggplant and salt well. Arrange cut side down on a baking sheet and roast for 20 minutes, or until tender. Cool slightly, then scoop the flesh into a bowl and mash. Set the skins aside.

2. MAKE THE FILLING: Mix together the lamb, grated onion and garlic, the fresh herbs, 2 teaspoons of the salt, and the spice blend in a bowl and set aside.

3. Heat the oil in a large skillet over medium-high heat. Add the bell peppers and a pinch of salt. Cook for 3 minutes, stirring constantly, then add the chopped onion and minced garlic and cook until translucent, about 8 more minutes. Add the meat mixture and cook for about 5 minutes, stirring to break up the meat. Add the tomato paste and crushed tomatoes. Mix well. Cook until the meat is no longer pink and the tomatoes have cooked down a bit, 3 to 5 minutes. Remove from the heat and stir in the mashed eggplant flesh.

4. Spoon the filling into the eggplant skins and top with the pine nuts. Pour the tomato sauce into a baking dish. Place the stuffed eggplant on top. Bake until heated through and the pine nuts are toasted, about 10 minutes. Spoon the sauce over the eggplant and serve.

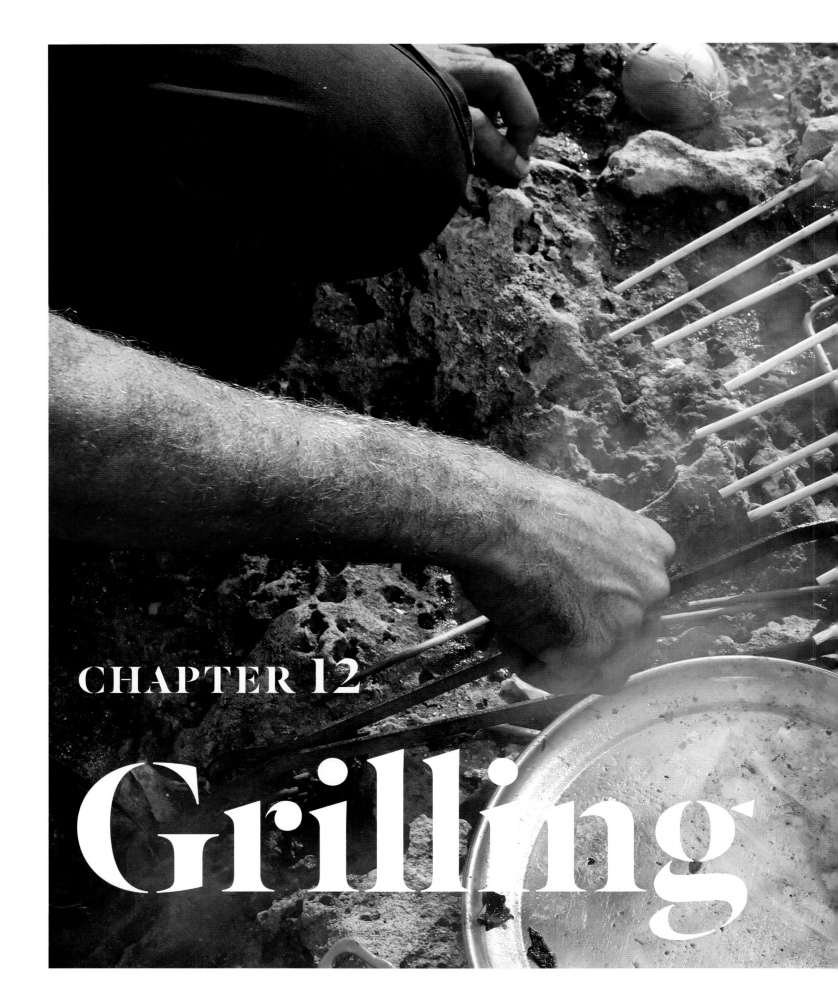

CHAPTER 12
Grilling

"You can't walk far before you're greeted by the seductive aroma of something delicious cooking over charcoal."

Not too long ago, Jerusalem's Machane Yehuda Market was a ghost town at night. When the sun went down, the produce vendors, butchers, and bakers closed up shop and hosed away the day's debris. In the darkness, the wet stone pavers reflecting light looked like the set of a noir film. For most of the market's century-plus existence, there was no activity in its warren of lanes and alleys after dark—at least not the human kind. Today it's another story: Machane Yehuda comes alive at night. It's a dinner destination.

The Morris brothers, David and Noam, grew up here. Their grandmother's apartment on Agrippas Street overlooks the market's main thoroughfare. Their father ran a restaurant here for over fifty years. Ten years ago the brothers opened a small storefront grill on butchers' row right in the middle of the market. They bought their meat a few kilos at a time, just enough to feed the four tables they could cram into the space. They served only lunch.

Dinner on the beach after work happens often. Here a couple from Haifa cooks lamb chops on their portable grill.

Then something began to happen in Machane Yehuda. Cafés and restaurants and bars popped up like mushrooms, adding a new dimension to this iconic center of commerce. People started coming at night. The roll-down gates securing the stalls became a walking gallery of edgy graffiti. Live music blared. People literally danced in the streets.

Today **Morris Restaurant** expands to up to 150 seats after dark, spilling out onto HeHaruv Street with folding tables covered in brightly patterned oilcloth. Young people kick back, drink beer, and shout at each other over the loud music that echoes in the partly covered, canyon-like alley, sharing a boisterousness with the platters of grilled meats that servers drop on tables already overflowing with hummus, pita, and salatim. The platters are unadorned; the charcoal-kissed meats glistening with fat speak for themselves. There is rich goose breast and beefy chunks of rib eye, spicy merguez sausage, and beef kofte kebabs, all imbued with the signature smoky aroma.

In the tiny kitchen, a single cook works furiously at a narrow grill. In one hand he holds a fistful of meat-laden metal skewers waiting for their turn over the fire. In the other hand, he grasps a hair dryer, brilliantly repurposed for stoking the coals. The same simple setup is found at countless restaurants and grills in Israel: an ingenious long, shallow stainless-steel trough full of charcoal in various stages of glow, with the skewers balancing on the edges.

The charcoal rewards patience. A good grill man will cook with coals that are ashen and almost completely burned out, and position them so close to the meat that they can whisper their intense heat without flaring up in the dripping fat.

You could probably find your way to Morris Restaurant blindfolded on the smell of charcoal smoke alone. Ditto for **M25**, Jonathan Borowitz's butcher's fantasy in the Carmel Market in Tel Aviv, where a similar after-hours awakening gives an afterlife to that shuk.

Charcoal cooking is at least as pervasive outside of restaurants, and quite literally outside. Israel is the size of New Jersey, with a roughly

equivalent population density and the major difference of a subtropical climate. Just replace *shopping malls* with *parks* and *beaches* and you get the extent to which outdoor living (and cooking) is a part of Israeli culture.

At a municipal park on a Saturday afternoon, charcoal grills dot the landscape like smoke signals. Extended families gather in the final hours of Shabbat for a *mangal*—the word refers to a barbecue as an event as well as the ubiquitous portable grills that fuel the party.

In the far north, on Achziv Beach National Park, just a few kilometers from the Lebanese border, a couple plays paddleball in the surf while children frolic in tidal pools. The beach is lined with graceful open-sided tents secured by sand bags, which provide temporary shelter for a day, or a week, at the beach. A shipping pallet is turned into a makeshift table, covered with a plastic cloth and set with a liter bottle of Coca-Cola and containers of store-bought prepared salads. Nearby a father balances a small charcoal grill on top of a rock, grilling skewers of cubed lamb.

The aroma stops us in our tracks.

It's not the sweet scent of hardwood, or the acrid odor of a tire fire. It's a clean smell, suggesting toasted spices, or charred fish skin, or chunks of marinated lamb; in other words, it smells like whatever happens to be cooking over it. More than hardwood smoke, charcoal harmonizes with its subject. It teases out and accentuates its essence. Its intense heat does its work quickly, leaving its subject better off than when it found it. If hardwood is the brash young cook who wants to transform every piece of food in the kitchen, charcoal is the mature chef who understands that restraint is often the best seasoning.

A father grilling lamb on the beach is joined by his son, a soldier who has driven hundreds of kilometers to spend a few precious hours with his family. The barbecue is the means, not the end—the journey, not the destination. It brings people together—at restaurants, parks, the beach, in the backyard, even on the side of the road. Sure, there are faster and more convenient ways to cook. But where is the joy in that?

SLICED GARLIC

CHOPPED PARSLEY

Building Kebabs

BAHARAT

KOSHER SALT

GRATED ONION

GROUND LAMB

A. Mix fatty ground lamb with spices and herbs.

B. Gently roll the lamb mixture between your palms to the desired shape.

C. Mold the lamb mixture around skewers, or shape into patties.

GROUND VEAL ON CINNAMON STICKS

BULGARIAN

ROMANIAN

MERGUEZ

ARABIC-STYLE

To Grill or Not

You may not always want to grill ground meat kebabs. Pan-frying or broiling are excellent options. First form the meat into balls about 2 inches in diameter and flatten each into a torpedo shape.

TO PAN-FRY: Heat a heavy skillet over medium-high heat and when the pan is very hot, add the kebabs in batches. Cook until the outsides are lightly charred and the centers are cooked through, 3 to 5 minutes per side.

TO BROIL: Preheat the broiler with a rack set 3 inches from the heating element. Place the kebabs on a wire rack set inside a rimmed baking sheet and broil until slightly charred on the outsides and cooked through, 3 to 5 minutes per side.

The heat is on at the shipudiya Itzik HaGadol in Jaffa, where masterful grill cooks juggle metal skewers of kebabs, offal, and even vegetables.

The Three Stages of Coal

1. UNLIT: Fill the grill with plenty of charcoal.

2. FIERY: Light and wait patiently for the flames to die down.

3. GRAY: Coals are at the perfect temperature to begin cooking.

Arabic-Style Kebabs

Serves 8

2½ pounds ground lamb (the fattier, the better)

1 tablespoon baharat

1½ teaspoons kosher salt

1 cup chopped fresh parsley

1 onion, grated

4 garlic cloves, thinly sliced

In the ancient Muslim Quarter of Jerusalem's Old City, there are still a few kebab stands with open hearths built into the walls and grill men who eschew utensils and tend to the kebabs with their asbestos hands.

That's our image when we hear the word *kebab*: ground lamb enhanced simply with baharat and onion, garlic, and parsley. The meat is traditionally cooked all the way through, so please use ground lamb with a high fat content (20 to 30 percent) to make sure the kebabs stay juicy. We inhaled these kebabs stuffed in a pita with only chopped salad and a pickle. They didn't even require tehina. We like to serve ours with Freekah Mujadara *(opposite)* and grilled onions and chiles.

1. Combine all the ingredients in a large bowl. Mix with your hands until well blended. Divide the mixture into 8 pieces, form each piece into a long, thin oval, and thread onto skewers. Refrigerate for 1 hour before cooking.

2. Grill the kebabs over indirect heat (or coals that have burned down to gray), or pan-fry or broil *(see page 266)*, until the outsides are lightly charred and the centers are cooked through, 5 to 7 minutes per side.

Freekah Mujadara

Serves 8

6 tablespoons olive oil

1 cup freekah

2 teaspoons plus a pinch of kosher salt

1 tablespoon Hawaij Spice Blend *(page 150)*

4½ cups water, plus more if needed

3 onions, sliced

4 garlic cloves, thinly sliced

1 cup black (or other) lentils

1 tablespoon baharat

Lemon juice

Most people know mujadara as a dish of lentils and rice, but the grain side of the equation is interchangeable and varies depending on where you are eating it. In the Galilee, wheat is a common stand-in for rice. Freekah is a type of cracked wheat that is harvested while still green. The process of removing the wheat berry involves burning away the rest of the plant, giving the freekah a smoky flavor that is a great complement to the sweet caramelized onions and earthy little black lentils.

1. Preheat the oven to 350°F. Heat 2 tablespoons of the olive oil in a large saucepan over medium-high heat. Add the freekah, 1 teaspoon of the salt, and the hawaij. Sauté for a few minutes, or until the grains are evenly coated. Remove from the heat, transfer to a baking dish (or a deep ovenproof pot with a lid), and add 2½ cups of the water. Cover tightly with foil. Bake until the freekah is tender and the water has been absorbed, about 45 minutes. Remove from the oven and keep covered for at least 10 minutes to steam.

2. Meanwhile, heat 2 tablespoons of the olive oil in a large skillet over medium heat. Add the onions and a pinch of salt and cook, stirring, until the onions are soft and translucent, about 5 minutes. Reduce the heat to medium-low and cook, stirring every few minutes, until the onions are caramelized, 30 to 45 minutes. (Lower the heat if the onions begin to burn; add a splash of water if they seem too dry.) Stir in the garlic and cook 2 minutes more. Set aside.

3. Put the lentils in a medium saucepan. Add the remaining 2 tablespoons olive oil, the remaining 1 teaspoon salt, and the baharat. Place the pan over medium-high heat, stir to coat the lentils, then cover with the remaining 2 cups water. Bring to a simmer, then reduce the heat to medium. Cook until the lentils are soft but not mushy, 30 to 40 minutes. Remove from the heat and drain.

4. Combine the lentils and freekah in a large bowl. Taste and add salt and lemon juice. Top with the caramelized onions and serve.

Romanian Kebabs

Serves 8

2½ pounds ground beef

8 garlic cloves, thinly sliced

1 tablespoon smoked paprika

1½ teaspoons kosher salt

1 teaspoon Espelette pepper

1 teaspoon crushed Aleppo pepper

2 tablespoons seltzer

1 teaspoon sugar

1 cup chopped fresh parsley

We love charcoal cooking so much we sometimes forget there are other perfectly legitimate cooking methods. But it takes time to prepare a proper charcoal fire, and it requires special ventilation or the ability to cook outdoors. And, of course, the grill is not the only or the best way to cook things. With all due respect to the flame-broiled Whopper, the best hamburgers are cooked on a griddle, where they develop a great crust while sizzling away in a slick of their own fat.

Even in Israel charcoal doesn't have a monopoly on kebab cookery. Plenty of restaurants have embraced a world of gas appliances and frying pans. Romanian and Bulgarian kebabs are two established mainstream players in Israel that you often encounter cooked on a griddle or in a pan.

Romanian kebabs are distinguished by their use of all ground beef and an unholy amount of garlic. A bit of sugar in the mix helps the kebabs brown evenly and form a nice crust in the pan. Adding a few tablespoons of seltzer helps the kebabs puff, making them lighter. Serve hot, with Carrot Chrain *(page 196)*.

1. Combine all the ingredients in a large bowl. Mix with your hands until well blended. Form into balls about 2 inches in diameter and thread onto skewers. Flatten each ball into a torpedo shape that hugs the skewer. Refrigerate for 1 hour before cooking.

2. Grill the kebabs over smoldering coals, or pan-fry or broil *(see page 266)*, until the outsides are lightly charred and the centers are cooked through, 3 to 5 minutes per side.

Romanian and Bulgarian kebabs flank a Moroccan fish stew at HaKosem in Tel Aviv.

Bulgarian Kebabs

Serves 8

1½ pounds ground beef
1 pound ground lamb
1½ onions, grated
2 teaspoons ground cumin
1½ teaspoons kosher salt
1 teaspoon smoked paprika
1 teaspoon freshly ground black pepper
1 teaspoon crushed Aleppo pepper
½ cup chopped fresh parsley
½ cup chopped fresh mint
2 tablespoons seltzer
1 teaspoon sugar

Bulgarian kebabs are a mix of beef and lamb, and they are traditionally offered in sweet or spicy versions depending on the cook's preference. This is the sweet version. Serve with Roasted Eggplant with Peppers *(page 191)*.

1. Combine all the ingredients in a large bowl. Mix with your hands until well blended. Form into balls about 2 inches in diameter and thread onto skewers. Refrigerate for 1 hour before cooking.

2. Grill the kebabs over smoldering coals, or pan-fry or broil *(see page 266)*, until the outsides are lightly charred and the centers are cooked through, 3 to 5 minutes per side.

Merguez Kebabs

Serves 8

2½ pounds ground lamb

Garlic cloves from 1 head, thinly sliced

2 teaspoons crushed Aleppo pepper

1½ teaspoons kosher salt

¼ teaspoon ground cardamom

¼ teaspoon fennel seed

¼ teaspoon ground cumin

¼ teaspoon ground coriander

¼ teaspoon ground caraway

½ cup chopped fresh parsley

½ cup chopped fresh cilantro

2 tablespoons seltzer

These spicy numbers come to us from North Africa, and versions of them are common in Morocco, Algeria, Tunisia, and Libya. They are also quite popular in France due to the historic French Colonial rule in the Maghreb. Besides the chile heat, which lends merguez its distinctive red color and piquancy, the spices are what distinguish these kebabs. The trio of cumin, coriander, and cardamom is a well-loved spice blend throughout the region, adding warm, sweet, and herbaceous notes to balance the richness of the lamb.

We tend to associate caraway with rye bread and European cooking, but it is widely used in North African cooking, and its anise-like notes add an extra-savory dimension to everything it touches. Eaten straight off the grill stuffed in a pita or over rice, merguez is also a traditional and indulgent addition to shakshouka, the North African baked egg dish that makes a killer brunch and/or hangover cure. Serve with the tomato-and-pepper salad Matbucha *(page 189)*.

1. Combine all the ingredients in a large bowl. Mix with your hands until well blended. Form into meatballs about 2 inches in diameter and thread onto skewers. Refrigerate for 1 hour before cooking.

2. Grill the kebabs over smoldering coals, or pan-fry or broil *(see page 266)*, until the outsides are lightly charred and the centers are cooked through, 3 to 5 minutes per side.

Morris Restaurant

JERUSALEM | When the Morris brothers, David and Noam *(above)*, opened their no-frills grill there over a decade ago, Machane Yehuda Market was a ghost town after dark. Today, it's a nightlife destination.

As the produce vendors stash their wares, the restaurant expands from its tiny storefront into the market's alleys. Guests sit at oilcloth-covered folding tables, feasting on skewers of meat grilled over charcoal. In the kitchen, a single cook manages to keep up, coaxing just the right amount of heat from the coals with a hair dryer.

A totally serious grill for the totally serious grilling that happens nightly at Jonathan Borowitz's M25 restaurant in Tel Aviv's Carmel Market.

Ground Veal on Cinnamon Sticks

Makes 16

2½ pounds ground veal

1 onion, grated

1½ teaspoons kosher salt

1 teaspoon smoked paprika

1 teaspoon Espelette pepper

1 teaspoon ground allspice

1 cup chopped fresh parsley

16 cinnamon sticks

Quick Tehina Sauce *(page 145)*

¼ cup pine nuts, lightly toasted

The great Palestinian chef Hussein Abbas of **Restaurant El Babour**, in Umm al-Fahm, prepares a signature dish involving lamb kebabs formed on cinnamon sticks. First he grills his kebabs, then he puts them in an earthenware bowl with grilled onions and tomatoes. He seals the bowl with a lid of bread dough and bakes the dish in the oven. When the bread is cut away tableside, the billowing steam carries the heady scent of cinnamon, grilled meat, and onions, which should be bottled as perfume.

Our homage to Kebab El Babour takes a much simpler approach, but it is delicious, and its presentation will delight your guests. We use veal because it marries particularly well with the sweetness of spices like cinnamon and allspice.

1. Combine all the ingredients except the cinnamon sticks, tehina sauce, and pine nuts in a large bowl. Mix with your hands until well blended. Divide the mixture into 16 pieces and form each into a football shape. Press the end of a cinnamon stick into the center of each and shape the meat around it, leaving an inch-long handle. Refrigerate for 1 hour before cooking.

2. Grill the kebabs over smoldering coals, or pan-fry or broil *(see page 266),* until the outsides are lightly charred and the centers are cooked through, 3 to 5 minutes per side. Serve with the tehina sauce and pine nuts.

Jonathan Borowitz, M25

TEL AVIV | The chef made his mark on the Israeli food scene at the late Café 48, with traditional European Jewish cuisine in a modern context. Now he pioneers butcher-to-table cooking at the bustling M25 Meatmarket, after-hours in the Carmel Market. Just steps away is the butcher shop where Jonathan and his team break down some fifteen whole cows a week.

To order at M25, walk to the butcher case at the front and point to the cut(s) of your choice. The dry-aged porterhouse cooked over charcoal is rich and beefy and everything you hope for, but there's a lot more than just steak. Don't sleep on the coarsely chopped beef liver with brains, onions, and cornichons, or the cabbage stuffed with intestines.

Sirloin Shishlik

Serves 8

3 pounds sirloin flap steak, fat removed, cut into 1-inch cubes

2 teaspoons kosher salt

MARINADE

1 onion, coarsely chopped

5 garlic cloves, peeled

1 teaspoon dill seed

1 cup chopped fresh dill

1 cup chopped fresh parsley

1 cup canola oil

Grilling is a great way to intensify the "beefiness" of lean beef. In this marinade, the onion and garlic caramelize over the coals, deepening the flavor of the meat. The marinade is versatile and works well with poultry, meaty fish, or even grilled vegetables. Serve with grilled tomatoes and a bowl of Everyday Schug *(page 151)*.

1. Toss the steak with the salt and thread onto skewers.

2. **MAKE THE MARINADE:** Put the onion, garlic, and dill seed in a blender and blend until the onion is very finely minced. Add the herbs a few handfuls at a time, blending between additions until the mixture looks smooth. With the motor running, slowly stream in the oil and blend until emulsified.

3. Pour the marinade into a large container that will fit the skewers. Add the skewers and turn to coat the meat. Cover and refrigerate for at least 3 hours or up to overnight.

4. Remove the skewers from the marinade and wipe the excess marinade from the meat. Grill directly over hot coals, or pan-fry or broil *(see page 266)*, turning every few minutes, until the meat is lightly charred and cooked through, about 8 minutes total.

Whole Butterflied Trout

Serves 4

1 whole trout, skin on and butterflied, spine removed (ask your fishmonger to do this)

1 teaspoon kosher salt

½ cup Classic Mango Amba (*page 79*) **or** store-bought

Grilled fish skin may be our favorite expression of charcoal. Here we grill whole butterflied trout (head and tail on, spine removed) almost entirely with the flesh side up, so that the skin gets bubbly, charred, and crispy. Then we briefly "kiss" the flesh side over the coals to caramelize the sweet-and-sour amba sauce. Serve with Pan-Roasted Green Beans *(page 171)*.

1. Sprinkle the trout on both sides with the salt and generously brush the amba on the flesh side.

2. Grill the fish over smoldering coals, skin side down, until almost completely cooked through, 7 to 8 minutes. You'll see the flesh slowly turn from translucent to opaque, starting at the edges and moving toward the center. Flip the fish and grill for 30 seconds to 1 minute.

Tunisian-Style Grilled Tuna

Serves 4

- 4 **(3- to 4-ounce) tuna steaks**
- 1 **teaspoon kosher salt**
- ½ **to 1 cup Fresh Harissa** *(page 150)* **or store-bought, plus more for serving**
- 1 **lemon, quartered**

Almost everyone loves grilled tuna. It is as deeply satisfying as any red meat but quite a bit leaner. The combination of tuna and harissa, the fiery North African chile condiment, is classically Tunisian, reflecting the country's Mediterranean coastline and subtropical climate. Any leftovers can be flaked apart and mixed with some mayonnaise spiked with additional harissa for a next-level tuna salad. Serve with Dill Tabbouleh *(page 195)*.

Sprinkle the tuna steaks with the salt and brush on both sides with up to 1 cup of harissa. Place the tuna on a rack directly over very hot coals and squeeze the lemon on top. Grill until the outsides of the tuna steaks have grill marks but the centers are still pink, about 2 minutes per side. Squeeze more lemon juice over the tuna. Serve with more harissa.

CHAPTER 13

Savory

"Israel's ready embrace of the culinary traditions of far-flung cultures has immeasurably enriched its own cuisine."

We are walking on a narrow, winding road in Tzfat (aka Safed, and pronounced something close to *svat*), about two hours north of Tel Aviv. The highest city in Israel and one of the oldest, this is the center of Jewish mysticism, and somehow, we feel it in the air. It is Friday, a few hours before Shabbat, and we smell something delicious wafting through a small doorway. Peering into a shallow room, we find **Fricassee Zahava**, literally a hole in the wall. To the left a tiny kitchen looks like it was ripped out of a motel efficiency thirty years ago. In fact not much has changed since the proprietress, Zahava Lagziel, opened her namesake restaurant in 1984, cooking the recipes her parents taught her after moving from Tunisia to Israel in 1959.

We watch as Zahava sets down a bowl before a man with a wild white beard and knit skullcap who looks like he does not need a meal. In the bowl is fresh couscous under a steaming vegetable tagine—the smell that first drew us in. The handmade couscous *(page 241)* is finely textured and moist, nothing like the instant version we buy in a box. Together with the tagine *(page 242)*, some harissa *(page 150)*, and chirshi *(page 196)*, the amazing

butternut squash condiment from the Barbary Coast, this is comfort food for the end of days.

With barely enough room in her kitchen to turn around, Zahava busies herself preparing for the Sabbath. She places a plate of fresh sfinj, powdered sugar–covered Moroccan donuts, on an oilcloth-covered table. Back in the kitchen, she rubs more fresh couscous through a giant sieve and braids challah. A dozen or so loaves of bread, shaped like small baguettes, sit on a nearby surface, proofed and ready to go into the oven—only they are not going into the oven. As we watch Zahava place a few loaves in a fryer basket and submerge them in hot oil, we realize we're about to experience the Tunisian fricassee.

Coastline comprises nearly half of Tunisia's borders, so the country's food has much in common with the maritime cuisines of other Mediterranean countries, including a healthy dose of olive oil, fish, and tomatoes. But it is also characterized by plenty of chile heat and North African spicing.

The Tunisian fricassee sandwich is emphatically not the French stew. In fact it has a very Provençal feel. With tuna, egg, potato, tomato, and olives,

Fricassee Zahava

TZFAT | Out of her tiny kitchen in Tzfat, an old city that winds down old streets into alleys and courtyards, Zahava Lagziel whips up a slew of delicacies from her native Tunisia, including hand-rolled couscous with stewed vegetables *(page 241)*.

Her fricassee, stuffed with hard-boiled egg, potato, olives, preserved lemon, harissa, and chirshi, is like a tuna hoagie from the imaginary Wawa on the Barbary Coast.

the sandwich was surely salade Niçoise in another life. The addition of preserved lemon, harissa, and chirshi are the only signs that we are not in Nice. Zahava includes fried eggplant and chopped pickles in her sandwich because, well, this is Israel. It is perfectly balanced, with no trace of greasiness from the fried bread.

The Jewish community in Tunisia dates back more than 2,000 years to the time of the Babylonian exile. An influx of Spanish Jews arrived after the Inquisition, and for the next several hundred years, the Tunisian Jewish community alternated between periods of prosperity and discrimination. The establishment of a French protectorate in the late nineteenth century was good for the Jews—and the food.

Zahava's husband, Shimon, has kept in the background, but when he sees our enthusiasm for the couscous and the fricassee, he beckons us into the kitchen and performs a magic trick: his brik. He spreads a spoonful of mashed potatoes in the center of a round of brik dough, a thin, crepe-like pancake. Next he drops a raw egg in the center of the potatoes and quickly folds the brik in half on itself. It magically seals into a half-moon as it plunges into a pot of oil. The brik emerges golden and crispy, with a runny egg trapped inside.

We encountered a similar brik at a stand in the Carmel Market in Tel Aviv: a Tunisian variation from the Ottoman boreka family. The stand consists mainly of a great wide pot filled with boiling oil and one man shouting, "Boreeka! Boreeka! Boreeka!" at passersby. That man performs the same trick as Shimon, but when he fishes the parcel out of the oil, he shoves the whole thing inside a waiting pita, adding chopped salad, cabbage, harissa, and chirshi. When he cuts the sandwich in half, the sound of the knife going through the crunchy brik is shattering. In a good way. This brik is the sandwich you never knew you were missing.

HaBoreeka

CARMEL MARKET | You could miss this tiny stand if the proprietor wasn't always shouting, "Boreeka! Boreeka!" loud enough to hear in Jerusalem. It's the dish so nice you have to say it twice—a crepe-like piece of brik dough folded around a raw egg, deep-fried, then stuffed into a pita with salad and North African condiments. The cost of the show is included.

Khachapuri

Makes 2 breads

2 cups crumbled feta cheese

1 cup grated kashkaval or mozzarella cheese

1 cup thinly sliced fresh chives

1 cup chopped fresh dill

2 balls pita dough (page 57)

2 large eggs

2 tablespoons unsalted butter

The collapse of the Soviet Union in the 1990s spurred a major wave of Georgian-Jewish immigration to Israel. Tango Sharvit arrived in 1992 at the age of thirteen. In 2009 he left his job to open **Khachapuria** in Jerusalem's Machane Yehuda Market, proudly serving the food of his youth. The success of the restaurant is yet another example of how Israel continues to absorb new arrivals and embrace their traditions as part of the nascent canon of their cuisine. When we last visited, Tango was behind the counter, stretching dough to order for khachapuri, Georgia's national bread, which is gaining popularity in the U.S. as well.

There are many variations of khachapuri, each based on a central theme of bread dough baked with cheese in the center. To eat it you tear off pieces of the bread and dip them in the cheese. What's not to like? The version here is called acharuli (to make two, we use half of our pita recipe): The bread is formed into a boat shape and an egg is baked in the center along with the cheese. Once it comes out of the oven, you add a pat of butter for good measure.

1. Place a baking stone or upside-down baking sheet on a rack in the bottom third of the oven and preheat to 500°F (or as hot as your oven can get). Mix together the feta, kashkaval or mozzarella, chives, and dill in a medium bowl and form into 2 balls.

2. On a floured surface, using your fingertips, press one ball of pita dough into an oval about 8 inches long and 6 inches wide. Press one cheese ball into the center of the dough and flatten it with your palm. Fold the dough up around the cheese and twist the ends to make a boat shape. Repeat with the second ball of dough and cheese ball. Use two spatulas or a pizza peel to transfer the breads to the stone or baking sheet in the oven.

3. Bake until the cheese is melted and the crust is light golden, 4 to 5 minutes, then crack an egg in the middle of each boat and continue baking for 2 to 3 minutes, or until the egg whites are just set.

4. Remove the breads from the oven and top each with 1 tablespoon of the butter. Serve hot.

Khachapuria

JERUSALEM | "All Georgians are proud of us," says Khachapuria owner Tango Sharvit, who brought the Georgian bread to Israel. There are many different types of khachapuri. This acharuli is filled with cheese, egg, and a healthy knob of butter, which is probably why I look so happy.

Yemenite Sabbath Bread: Kubaneh, Jachnun, and Malawach

Whenever someone asks me to recommend restaurants in Israel, I encourage them to try to get themselves invited to someone's house. Shabbat dinner in an Israeli home? That's the best meal in Israel. Shabbat breakfast in a Yemenite household may be a close second.

So much of Jewish cooking is distinguished by what happens just before sundown on Friday night. By rabbinical fiat, ovens and hot plates may remain on, but all cooking must cease. This practice has given rise to numerous slow-cooked stews, assembled and popped into the oven just as the Sabbath begins. Hamin, cholent, fafina, t'bit: Almost every Jewish culture has its version of a one-pot, nap-inducing Shabbat lunch, hot and ready when the family returns from synagogue.

Yemenite cooks have done something similar for breakfast, working magic with dough, transforming the humblest of ingredients into delicacies fit for kings. Kubaneh, jachnun, and malawach form a Venn diagram of breads. Kubaneh and jachnun are different doughs that are cooked in the same manner: overnight in a low oven and ready for a rich Shabbat breakfast before heading off to synagogue. Jachnun and malawach are made from the same dough, cooked two different ways.

It is rare to encounter kubaneh and jachnun in Israeli restaurants, so it is special to be able to sample them in a private home. Once, on a culinary tour of Israel, I learned that our bus driver was married to a Yemenite woman. We immediately turned the bus around and drove to his house. After a brief whispered conversation with her husband, she proceeded to take us into her kitchen and teach us the way she makes jachnun.

On a Saturday morning during a recent visit to Tel Aviv, we ducked into a small apartment a few blocks from the beach. The living quarters of a Yemenite family had been converted into a sort-of restaurant. Two folding tables with plastic chairs were wedged into the living room. In the kitchen,

Adeena Sussman

TEL AVIV | In addition to making the best kubaneh ever, Adeena is a knowledgeable food writer, cook, and host. Since she moved from New York (and married Jay Shofet, *below*), she's become a very cool advocate for Israel's diverse and evolving foodways. Her apartment is near the Carmel Market, and her commitment to cooking locally and seasonally—beautifully documented on Instagram and in her writing—is a huge inspiration to us.

Tucked into a tiny Tel Aviv apartment a few steps off the street is the improbably informal Jachnun by the Sea.

family members peeled eggs and pulled pans of kubaneh and jachnun out of a small home oven. In the space between the kitchen and dining room, two men sat on either side of a wide desk, chatting and warily eyeing us as we entered and tried to make sense of what was happening.

We squeezed into some seats and ordered one of everything on the menu: jachnun and malawach. Jachnun uses a laminated dough similar to puff pastry. After it's rolled out, it's rolled up again in a tight rope and coiled in a special covered aluminum tin in which it bakes and caramelizes overnight at a low temperature. The result is dense, chewy, buttery, and sweet. You take a piece of jachnun, unroll it, and add some grated tomato and a dollop of schug. Then you roll it back up and pop it in your mouth before the condiments drip down your arm. Eggs that have been baked overnight in their shells in the same tin as the jachnun are a must-have accompaniment.

Kubaneh is a yeasted dough enriched with butter. It has a small amount of sugar, but nowhere near enough to account for the alchemy that occurs under the gentle, persistent heat of the overnight bake. The deep mahogany-colored bread that emerges has a steamy, soft interior with notes of molasses and honey and a satisfyingly chewy crust. It is difficult to comprehend that all-purpose flour is responsible for a flavor that is so complex and wheat-y.

Mostly these are home-cooked breads, with the exception of malawach. Thanks, in part, to the Arcovi family, owners of my beloved Opera, a Yemenite restaurant in Hadera, malawach is now a frozen commercial product that is available in Israeli restaurants, supermarkets, and even here in America! It also uses a laminated dough. Small pieces of the rolled-out dough are shallow-fried until they brown and puff into gloriously crispy exteriors with rich and chewy interiors. Since it is fried to order, malawach is not a particularly Sabbath-friendly dish. But its obvious appeal has allowed it to break into the Israeli mainstream, where it is served in both traditional (with hard-boiled eggs, grated tomato, and schug) and nontraditional (as a sandwich wrapper) ways.

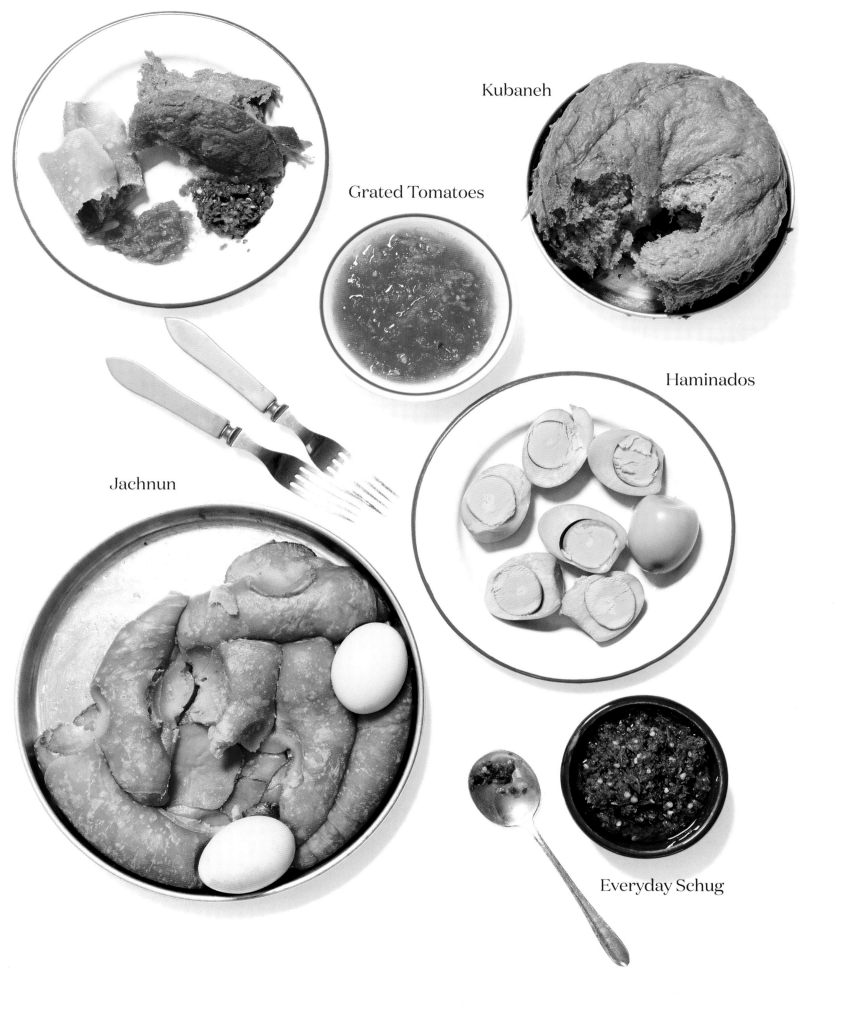

Kubaneh

Grated Tomatoes

Haminados

Jachnun

Everyday Schug

Jachnun

Makes 1 bread

4 cups all-purpose flour

2 tablespoons kosher salt

2 tablespoons sugar

½ teaspoon baking powder

2 tablespoons white vinegar

1¾ cups water

16 tablespoons (2 sticks) unsalted butter, at room temperature

1 large Yukon Gold potato, thinly sliced

4 eggs

This unleavened laminated dough creates a bread with thin layers that are rich, dense, and chewy. Jachnun (like kubaneh) gets wonderful complexity from its slow overnight bake. There is no better aroma to wake up to on a Saturday morning. Serve with Everyday Schug *(page 151)*, Grated Tomatoes *(opposite)*, and the eggs it bakes with.

1. Combine the flour, salt, sugar, baking powder, vinegar, and water in the bowl of a stand mixer fitted with the dough hook. Mix on low speed until the dough comes together and begins to pull away from the bowl, then mix for 3 more minutes. Divide the dough in two and return to the bowl. Cover with plastic wrap and set aside to rest for 30 minutes at room temperature.

2. Scrape out 1 piece of the dough and roll it out on a large cutting board to the size of the board. (Don't worry about making it perfect.) Spread half the butter to cover the dough. Starting at a short end, roll the dough up as tightly as you can into a sausage shape. Repeat with the remaining dough and butter. Refrigerate the dough rolls for 1 hour.

3. Line the bottom of a 9-inch spring-form pan or high-sided cake pan with the potato slices. Cut each dough roll into 4 pieces and arrange the 8 pieces in the prepared pan. Place the whole eggs, still in their shells, on top.

4. Cover and let the dough rise at room temperature for 30 minutes or for up to 4 hours in the refrigerator. (If refrigerated, let it return to room temperature for 30 minutes before baking.)

5. Preheat the oven to 250°F. Bake the jachnun for 8 hours, or until deep golden brown. Let cool to room temperature, then peel and halve the eggs. Serve the bread with the eggs, Everyday Schug, and Grated Tomatoes.

Kubaneh

Makes 1 bread

1¼ teaspoons active dry yeast

¼ cup sugar

1¼ cups warm water

4 cups all-purpose flour

1 tablespoon kosher salt

12 tablespoons (1½ sticks) unsalted butter, at room temperature, plus more for the rolling pin and pan

Our recipe makes a kubaneh that rises as one long, coiled roll. But a "monkey bread" style of smaller coiled rolls is also a common presentation. To make the bread this way, slice the rolled coil into even cross sections and nestle them in a pot, cut side up and side by side. Serve with Everyday Schug *(page 151)* and Grated Tomatoes.

1. Combine the yeast and sugar with the water in the bowl of a stand mixer fitted with the dough hook. Let sit for 6 to 8 minutes, or until foamy. Add the flour and salt. Mix on low speed for 4 minutes, then increase the speed to high and mix for 4 more minutes. Cover and let the dough rise for 2 hours at room temperature, until it doubles in volume, or refrigerate overnight. (If refrigerated, let it return to room temperature 1 hour before baking.)

2. Spread the butter evenly on a large cutting board with a silicone or offset spatula. Butter your rolling pin and the inside of a medium ovenproof pot or covered casserole dish. Scrape the dough onto the buttered surface and roll it out to the size of your board. (Don't worry about making it perfect.) Starting at a short end, roll the dough up as tightly as you can and coil it into a sausage-like spiral. Place the dough in the prepared pot.

3. Cover and let rise at room temperature for 30 minutes or in the refrigerator for up to 4 hours. (If the dough is refrigerated, let it return to room temperature for 30 minutes before baking.)

4. Preheat the oven to 250°F. Bake the kubaneh, covered, for 8 hours, or until deep golden brown.

Grated Tomatoes *(Resek)*

Makes about 2 cups

Blanch 2 pounds tomatoes in boiling water for 1 minute, then shock them in a bowl of ice water. Peel off and discard the skins and grate the tomatoes into a medium bowl. Add a big pinch of kosher salt and a drizzle of olive oil, and serve.

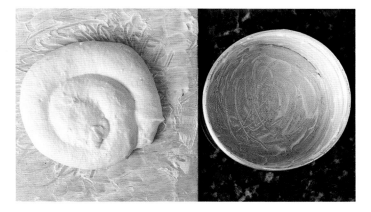

Malawach

Makes 8 large or 16 small pieces

6¼ cups all-purpose flour

2 tablespoons kosher salt

2 tablespoons sugar

½ teaspoon baking powder

1 tablespoon distilled white vinegar

1¾ cups water

12 tablespoons (1½ sticks) unsalted butter, at room temperature, plus more for the rolling pin

Canola oil, for frying

Like its cousins kubaneh and jachnun, malawach requires some advance planning. The upside is that the dough keeps indefinitely in the freezer and is cooked from frozen, so you're never more than a few minutes away from a malawach celebration. Serve hot with labneh and jam.

1. Combine the flour, salt, sugar, baking powder, vinegar, and water in the bowl of a stand mixer fitted with the dough hook. Mix on low speed until the dough comes together and begins to pull away from the bowl, then mix for 3 more minutes. Cover the bowl with plastic wrap and let rest for 30 minutes at room temperature.

2. Spread the butter evenly on a large cutting board with a silicone or offset spatula. Butter your rolling pin. Scrape the dough onto the buttered surface and roll it out to the size of your board. (Don't worry about making it perfect.) Starting at a short end, roll the dough up as tightly as you can and coil it into a sausage-like spiral. Refrigerate the dough, covered, on the board for 1 hour, then roll the dough out again to a large rectangle, roll it up,

and shape it into a spiral. Refrigerate, covered, for 1 hour. Repeat this process once more, ending with another hour in the refrigerator.

3. Divide the dough into 8 large or 16 small pieces and roll them out into circles the size of your skillet. Separate the circles with pieces of parchment paper and stack on a parchment-lined baking sheet. Freeze, covered, overnight.

4. The next day, add about ⅛-inch canola oil to a large cast-iron skillet and place over medium-high heat. When the oil is hot, add a piece of frozen dough and fry until puffy and golden brown on the bottom, about 3 minutes, then flip and fry for 2 more minutes. Repeat with the remaining dough, adding oil as needed.

A. Fry the frozen dough on one side until fluffy, like a large, flaky pancake.

B. The finished malawach is a crispy treat to sop up soups or stews, or to spread with jam.

Tzfat is the highest city in Israel and is said to have mystical power. Narrow stone passageways lead to art galleries and shops.

Jerusalem Bagels

Makes 6 small or 8 large

1 packet active dry yeast

3 tablespoons sugar

1¾ cups warm water

4 cups bread flour

⅓ cup canola oil

⅓ cup labneh

1½ teaspoons kosher salt

1 tablespoon baking soda

2 large eggs

Sesame seeds, for sprinkling

Jerusalem bagels have much in common with regular bagels. Both have a hole in the middle, and both are often covered in sesame seeds, but that's where the similarities end. Unlike the common bagel, Jerusalem bagels are not boiled before baking, so they are tender and fluffy where regular bagels are dense and chewy. Their ingredient list often includes milk or milk powder and sugar, making them slightly sweet as well.

When I step inside the gates of the Old City of Jerusalem, I have to eat one of these bagels immediately. The oblong, sesame-covered rings are everywhere. You see them threaded on long wooden dowels slung over the shoulders of street hawkers, and piled high on wooden trays at bakeries and market stalls.

The origin of the name is unclear. It is most likely a rebranding of ka'ak, the sesame-covered bread ring popular in the Middle East and widely considered to be a specialty of Jerusalem. One theory is that European Jews encountered ka'ak for the first time after Israel captured the Old City during the Six-Day War in 1967. Given their similarity to the bagels they knew from back home (bagels were invented in Poland sometime before the seventeenth century), the Jerusalem bagel (or the more affectionate, Yiddish-inflected *baygeleh*) was a logical name.

Jerusalem bagels are traditionally served very simply, with savory and salty za'atar wrapped in a scrap of old newspaper. Rip off a chunk and dip it in the za'atar—or dunk it first in a little dish of olive oil.

Israelis have enlisted Jerusalem bagels for a whole new category of sandwiches. Toastim, Jerusalem bagels stuffed with sandwich ingredients and pressed like panini, are an Israeli café and coffee shop staple. The slightly sweet bread toasts up beautifully and is a great match for such savory fillings as olive butter with feta and tomato, and cured salmon with labneh and avocado.

This is a super-simple and rewarding bread to make at home. And since we're in Philly, home of the soft pretzel, we've taken Jerusalem bagels

e Mount / Al-Haram Al-Sharif

הכותל המערבי
الحائط المغربي
The Western Wall

כנסיית הקבר
كنيسة القيامة
of the Holy Sepulchre

In the venerable alleyways of Jerusalem's Old City, tables of Jerusalem bagels are everywhere.

one step further by "pretzel-izing" them. Pretzels get their unique flavor and texture from a dip in a lye solution prior to baking. But lye is a hazardous, slightly scary chemical that's not readily available. Fortunately, baking soda is similarly alkaline, so now you can "pretzel-ize" worry-free in your own kitchen.

1. Combine the yeast, sugar, and 1½ cups of the water in the bowl of a stand mixer fitted with the dough hook. Let sit until foamy, about 5 minutes. Add the flour, oil, labneh, and salt and mix until the dough comes together. Cover the bowl and let rise at room temperature until it almost doubles in volume, 1 to 1½ hours. Portion the dough into 6 to 8 equally sized balls and place on a lightly floured large board. Cover with a kitchen towel and let rest at room temperature for 1 hour.

2. Pat one piece of dough into a rough rectangle the size of your board, then roll it up, starting from one long end, pinching and deflating/degassing the dough as you roll. Pinch the seam to seal. Continue rolling the dough into a long rope using both hands, starting in the middle and moving outward to make it as even as

possible (it should be about 1½ feet long). Bring the edges together to make a long oval and pinch to seal. Repeat with the remaining dough pieces. Let rise on the board for 1 hour. The dough will puff up a bit.

3. Preheat the oven to 350°F. Line two baking sheets with parchment paper. Spread out the baking soda in a small ovenproof dish and bake for 3 minutes. Remove from the oven and whisk with the eggs and the remaining ¼ cup water in a small bowl. After the dough ovals have risen, place them on the prepared baking sheets. Brush the tops with the egg wash, using all of it, and sprinkle liberally with sesame seeds. Bake until deep golden brown, 12 to 15 minutes.

A. Each Jerusalem bagel starts as a ball of dough. Roll it into a thin rope about 1½ feet long.

B. Form the signature long, oval bagel shape by joining the ends of the rope.

C. Proof the long oval pieces on a board for 1 hour. They'll puff up a bit.

D. Brush the proofed dough with egg wash, then sprinkle with lots of sesame seeds.

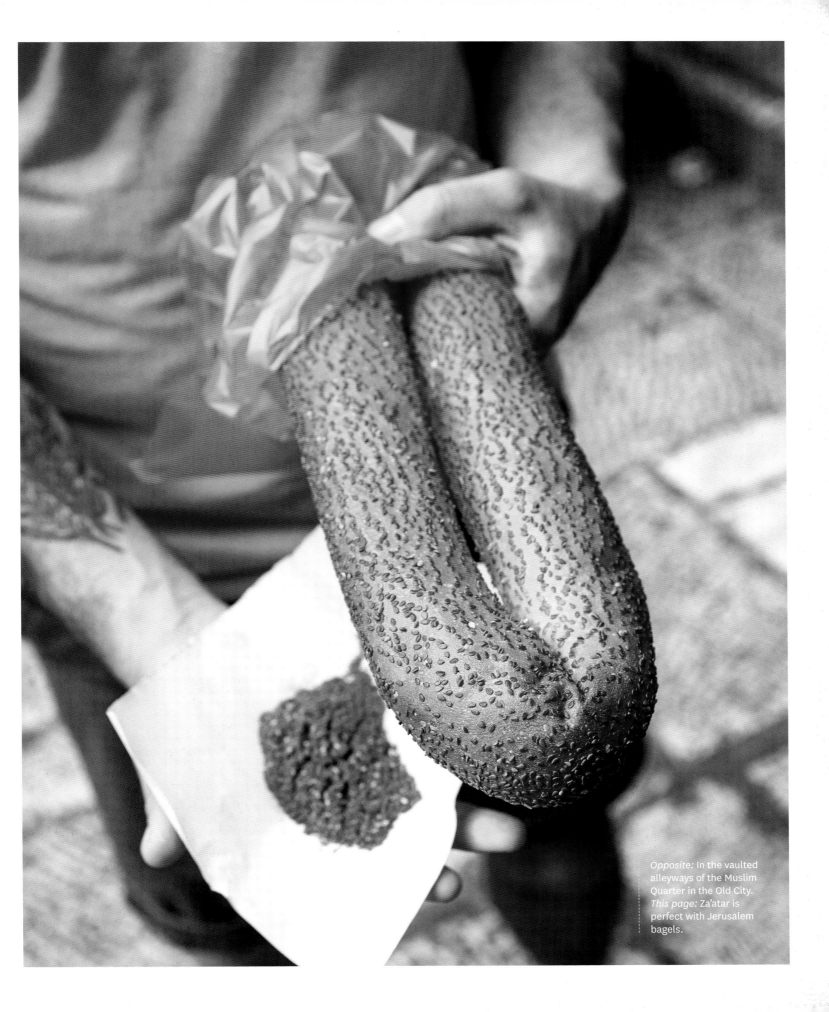

Opposite: In the vaulted alleyways of the Muslim Quarter in the Old City. *This page:* Za'atar is perfect with Jerusalem bagels.

Olive Butter, Feta, and Tomato Toastim

For each sandwich, spread both halves of a split Jerusalem Bagel *(page 300)* with a generous amount of Olive Butter. Sprinkle half of the bagel with crumbled feta cheese and add some sliced pitted green olives. Place thinly sliced tomato on the other half and sprinkle with za'atar. Close the sandwich. Place a cast-iron skillet over medium-high heat. Drop a tablespoon of butter into the hot skillet and let it melt. Add the sandwich, press it down with another skillet, and cook until the bagel is browned and the olive butter begins to melt, about 2 minutes. Flip, press it down, and cook until the cheese has melted and the other side is browned, 2 minutes more.

Olive Butter

Makes about 1½ cups

16 tablespoons (2 sticks) unsalted butter, at room temperature
½   cup pitted green olives

Combine the butter and olives in a food processor and process until smooth.

Salmon, Labneh, and Avocado Sandwich

For each sandwich, spread some labneh on the bottom half of a split Jerusalem Bagel *(page 300)*. Slice half an avocado and place the slices on top of the labneh, followed by thinly sliced Cured Salmon *(page 308)*. Sprinkle with salt and top with the other half of the bagel.

Cured Salmon

Serves 8

2 pounds salmon fillets, pin bones removed

2 tablespoons kosher salt

1½ tablespoons sugar

Grated zest of 1 grapefruit

½ cup grapefruit juice

¼ cup arak

Fresh dill

We love this three-day cure of salmon in arak, the anise-flavored grape distillate popular throughout the eastern Mediterranean and especially Lebanon, whose many wineries make some of the best. As a drink, it's traditionally poured over ice (which turns it milky white) and sipped with mezze. Although arak is increasingly available in the U.S., if you can't find it, raki, ouzo, or pastis will work their magic, too.

Place the salmon in a baking dish. Combine the salt, sugar, grapefruit zest and juice, and arak in a small bowl. Rub this mixture onto the salmon on both sides. Cover with plastic wrap and refrigerate for 3 days. Unwrap, rinse the fish, and transfer to a clean dish. Refrigerate, uncovered, overnight. Slice thinly and scatter on dill sprigs. The salmon will keep for 1 week, refrigerated.

This Is One Flaky Pastry

Borekas are in the family of filled savory pastries that spread throughout the Levant, Balkans, and Mediterranean over five hundred years of Ottoman rule.

Sephardic immigrants like my Bulgarian grandmother popularized borekas in Israel after World War II. Now they are sold just about everywhere you might be hungry—bakeries, coffee shops, supermarket freezer cases, roadside kiosks. Borekas were one of the first foods that moved me as a young, picky eater, and my first kitchen job was to make them, so it's not a stretch to say that borekas launched my career. I still get excited about making (and eating) them today.

There are dozens of regional variations of boreka—also commonly called *borek* or *brik*, or some close equivalent—throughout the former Ottoman Empire. Some versions are made from sheets of phyllo dough brushed with oil. But many Israeli borekas, including my grandmother's, use a laminated dough, which has lots of thin layers of fat (e.g., butter) interspersed with thin layers of dough. When the boreka dough meets the intense heat of the oven, the water in the butter turns to steam, separating the dough into a multitude of flaky layers. The same principle is at work in puff pastry and croissants.

Laminated dough is a simple concept in theory, but making it can be painstaking and time-consuming. Even professionals avoid it or relegate it to specialists with the right machinery to make the process efficient. At our Philadelphia bakery, **K'far**, we use a commercial machine called a sheeter to produce fresh borekas every morning. The sheeter consists of a set of rollers mounted on top of a long conveyor belt. Between folds the dough is run back and forth through the rollers to create a precise, even thickness so we can quickly create large batches of borekas.

Borekas Ramle

JERUSALEM | Located at the top of Machane Yehuda Market, Borekas Ramle represents the old school. It's not a bakery—it's a stand selling huge, flaky Turkish-style borekas. With pickles, tehina, schug, and a hard-boiled egg, this boreka is a meal in itself.

Borekas

Makes 24 small or 6 large pastries

2 cups all-purpose flour, plus more for rolling

1 tablespoon olive oil

1 teaspoon apple cider vinegar

1 tablespoon kosher salt

Scant cup seltzer, plus more as needed

8 tablespoons (1 stick) unsalted butter, softened

1 egg, for brushing

In the *Zahav* cookbook, we laid out a three-day process to make borekas by hand. We know what you're thinking: *What were they thinking?* Frankly, borekas are not something that gainfully employed people make often, especially when their jobs do not involve making borekas. In a weak moment, we even admit you can, in fact, use store-bought all-butter puff pastry sheets.

If you want great borekas outside of Israel, you pretty much have to make them yourself. So we've developed an ingenious method that can be done start to finish in under two hours. It may not be as quick as 5-Minute Hummus *(page 145)*, but on a relative basis, it's every bit as big of a breakthrough.

1. Combine the flour, oil, vinegar, and salt in a food processor, then add the seltzer. Process until the mixture looks crumbly, then continue for a few minutes more, adding a drop or two more of seltzer until the dough comes together in a ball. Process for 10 seconds, then flour the largest cutting board you have and scrape all the dough onto it. (You can also make the dough by hand in a large bowl with a wooden spoon.)

2. Press the dough into a rectangle about 6 inches long. (The dough is easiest to work with the closer you get to a perfect rectangle.) Flour your rolling pin and roll the dough out to the size of your cutting board, starting in the center and rolling in a fluid motion, moving your arms and applying gentle pressure instead of pressing down. When you're about halfway there, roll up the dough on the rolling pin, set aside, and flour the board again. Unroll the dough on the board.

3. Place the stick of butter on one end of the dough and, using a butter knife or silicone or offset spatula, spread it evenly in long motions over half the dough, leaving a ½-inch border on the edges.

4. Fold the unbuttered half of the dough over the buttered half. Fold the edges up and in to keep the butter inside. Fold the right and left edges into the center of the dough and fold in half again to make a book fold. *(See Steps I and J, page 316.)*

5. Sprinkle a bit of flour on the board, then pat the dough down into a perfect rectangle. It should feel smooth. Transfer the dough to the freezer (right on the cutting board, uncovered) for 15 minutes.

6. Remove the board from the freezer and gently press a finger into the dough. It should feel pliable. If you feel a shard of butter, it has hardened too much, so leave the dough out for a few minutes. You want the dough and the butter to be close to the same temperature so the butter doesn't crack and they roll out smoothly together.

7. Working quickly and with just enough flour to keep the dough from sticking to the board and rolling pin, roll the dough out to the size of the cutting board. If the dough sticks to the board, roll it up on the rolling pin, dust the board with more flour, and flip the dough. Sprinkle a little flour on any holes and continue rolling.

8. Fold the short ends in to meet in the center, then fold the whole thing in half again to create another book fold. Scrape off and discard any extra butter or flour from the board. Pat the dough into a perfect, even rectangle. It should still feel cold.

9. Return the dough to the freezer for 15 minutes. Repeat this process of making a book fold three more times, freezing it for 15 minutes between each new fold. You will roll out the dough five times total. Add only as much flour as needed to prevent the dough from sticking to the board and rolling pin.

10. After the last roll-out and freezing, remove the dough from the freezer. Dust it with flour on both sides, then roll it out one last time to fit the dimensions of the board. Cut the dough into roughly 3-inch squares (about 24) for small borekas or 6-inch squares (about 6) for large borekas. Place the squares on parchment paper–lined baking sheets, cover, and return to the freezer for another 15 minutes, or up to 5 days.

11. Preheat the oven to 400°F. Remove the dough from the freezer. (If frozen for longer than 15 minutes, let it thaw for 10 minutes, or until the squares are pliable.)

12. Whisk the egg in a small bowl. For small borekas, spoon a little of your chosen filling into the center of each square, brush the edges lightly with egg wash, and fold the dough over to make triangles or rectangles. For large borekas, drop a spoonful or two of filling just inside one corner of each square, brush the edges lightly with the egg wash, and fold the dough over to make triangles. Gently press the edges to adhere. Brush the tops with egg wash and sprinkle with seeds. Refrigerate on the baking sheet for 15 minutes.

13. Transfer the borekas to the oven. Bake small borekas for about 25 minutes, larger ones for about 30 minutes, rotating the baking sheet halfway through, until the dough puffs slightly and the tops are golden brown.

A. Mix all the ingredients in a food processor, then add the seltzer.

B. Process until the dough comes together, then turn it out onto a floured cutting board.

C. With your fingers, press the dough into a 6-inch-long rectangle.

D. Flour a rolling pin and roll out the dough in a fluid motion, moving yourself over the board.

E. Spread the butter over half the dough, leaving a ½-inch border.

F. Fold the unbuttered half over the buttered half; fold the edges in to keep the butter inside.

G. Pat the dough into a perfect rectangle on the board; transfer the dough on the board to the freezer.

H. In 15 minutes, remove from the freezer. Check that the butter and dough are the same temperature, then roll out.

I. Fold the short ends of the dough in to meet at the center.

J. Fold the dough in half again, so that the top folds over the bottom fold.

K. Pat the dough into an even rectangle; it should still feel cold.

L. Return the dough on the board to the freezer. Repeat this process three more times.

M. Remove the dough from the freezer, dust with flour, then roll out again to the dimensions of the board.

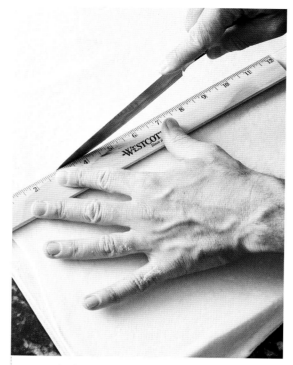

N. Cut the dough on the board into 3-inch squares for small borekas and 6-inch squares for large ones.

O. Once more into the freezer for 15 minutes (or up to 5 days to delay the process).

P. Spoon filling onto each dough square, brush the edges with the egg wash, fold into triangles, and press to seal.

Tomato Filling

- 2 tablespoons olive oil
- 1 small onion, minced
- 2 garlic cloves, thinly sliced
- Kosher salt
- ½ red bell pepper, seeded and finely chopped
- 3 large tomatoes, chopped
- Generous ½ cup shredded kashkaval or provolone cheese
- Black sesame seeds, for topping

1. Heat the oil in a medium saucepan over medium-high heat. Add the onion, garlic, and a pinch of salt, cook for 2 minutes, then add the bell pepper. Cook, stirring frequently, for 8 to 10 minutes, or until the vegetables are soft. Add the tomatoes and cook uncovered for 30 minutes, stirring every 5 minutes or so, until most of the liquid has evaporated and the mixture resembles a chunky sauce. Remove the pan from the heat and let the sauce cool to room temperature. Taste for salt and mix in the cheese.

2. Before baking, spoon filling onto the dough squares, brush the edges with egg wash, fold into triangles, press to seal the edges, and top with a sprinkling of black sesame seeds.

Eggplant Filling

- 1 large eggplant, halved lengthwise
- 2 tablespoons olive oil, plus more for seasoning
- Kosher salt
- Paprika
- 1 medium onion, minced
- 1 large red bell pepper, finely chopped
- 2 garlic cloves, thinly sliced
- ¼ cup chopped fresh mint
- Poppy seeds, for topping

1. Preheat the oven to 375°F. Score the eggplant with a few long, ¼-inch-deep cuts. Place on a baking sheet, cut side up, and season generously with olive oil, salt, and paprika. Roast for 40 minutes, or until the eggplant is tender. Let cool.

2. Heat the olive oil in a medium skillet over medium-high heat. Add the onion, pepper, and garlic and sauté for 8 to 10 minutes, or until the vegetables are soft. Let cool.

3. Scoop the eggplant flesh into a medium bowl. Add the onion-pepper mixture and mix well. Add the mint and taste for salt.

4. Before baking, spoon filling onto the dough squares, brush the edges with egg wash, fold into triangles, press to seal, and top with a sprinkling of poppy seeds.

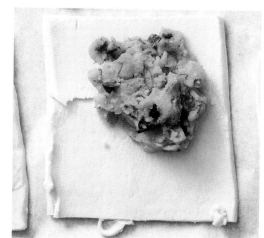

Each boreka filling recipe will make enough for 4 large or 8 small borekas.

Kale and Feta Filling

- 2 tablespoons olive oil
- 1 medium onion, minced
- 3 garlic cloves, thinly sliced
- Kosher salt
- 3 cups baby kale, finely chopped
- ⅓ cup crumbled feta cheese
- 1 large egg
- Nigella seeds, for topping

1. Heat the olive oil in a medium saucepan over medium-high heat. Add the onion, garlic, and a pinch of salt and cook for 8 to 10 minutes, or until the onion is soft and translucent. Add the kale and cook, tossing, just until it wilts. Transfer to a bowl and let cool. Sprinkle the feta over the kale mixture and combine. Taste and add salt. Crack the egg into a bowl, add the kale-feta mixture, and mix well.

2. Before baking, spoon filling onto the dough squares, brush the edges with egg wash, fold into triangles, press to seal the edges, and top with a sprinkling of nigella seeds.

Potato and Olive Filling

- 1 large Yukon Gold potato, peeled and cut into 1-inch chunks
- 2 tablespoons chopped pitted black olives
- 1 large egg, hard-boiled and crumbled
- ¼ cup chopped fresh dill
- Hawaij Spice Blend (page 150)
- Kosher salt
- Sesame seeds, for topping

1. Put the potato in a medium pot and cover with cold salted water by an inch or two. Bring to a boil over medium-high heat, then reduce the heat to medium-low and simmer for 15 minutes, or until the potato is fork-tender. Drain, cool, and transfer the potato to a bowl. Add the olives, egg, and dill and mash with a fork until the mixture is creamy (some lumps are fine). Taste and add hawaij and salt.

2. Before baking, spoon filling onto the dough squares, brush the edges with egg wash, fold into triangles, press to seal the edges, and top with a sprinkling of sesame seeds.

Boreka Sandwiches

Since Israelis have a passion for stuffed foods and for sandwiches, stuffing a boreka and turning it into a sandwich should be considered a double mitzvah. Baked with the right filling, sliced open, and enhanced with the appropriate ingredients, a boreka sandwich combines comforting warmth and vibrant, fresh flavors.

TO MAKE BOREKA SANDWICHES: Bake large borekas and let cool slightly. Split with a sharp knife, but don't cut them all the way through. Here we give suggestions, but almost any filling goes.

1. FOR SABICH-STYLE BOREKA SANDWICHES: Start with borekas with Eggplant Filling *(page 318)* and layer with sliced hard-boiled egg, Amba Tehina *(page 319)*, and sliced tomato.

2. FOR TUNISIAN-STYLE BOREKA SANDWICHES: Start with borekas with Potato and Olive Filling *(page 319)* and layer with flaked tuna, sliced tomato, chopped Quick Pickled Lemons *(page 201)*, black olives, and harissa.

3. FOR PIZZA-STYLE BOREKA SANDWICHES: Start with borekas with Tomato Filling *(page 318)* and make pizza-like layers with shredded or sliced cheese, anchovies, sautéed bell peppers, and a pickled shipka pepper.

4. FOR CALIFORNIA-STYLE BOREKA SANDWICHES: Start with borekas with Kale and Feta Filling *(page 319)* and layer with sliced tomato, sliced avocado, Quick Tehina Sauce *(page 145)*, and Everyday Schug *(page 151)*.

Borekas Penso

TEL AVIV | In the heart of Levinsky Market, at #43, Jenny Penso's shop is one of my favorite places to pick up a greasy bag of flaky borekas as soon as I land in Israel. Jenny makes their dough fresh every morning. She also uses it for konafi, highlighting the Ottoman connection between Turkish borekas and Arabic pastries.

1. Sabich-Style

2. Tunisian-Style

3. Pizza-Style

4. California-Style

CHAPTER 14

Sweet

FROM THE BAKERY

"As kids in Akko, we'd wait at the ovens for fresh pita, then we'd stuff konafi inside and eat it."

—OSAMA DALAL, CHEF

Pastries are part of the landscape in Israel—some are made so sweet, they're served with two glasses of water. As the king of Middle Eastern desserts, konafi is the poster child for this phenomenon. So it was all the more thrilling when chef Osama Dalal led us into the **Kashash** bakery in the Old City of Akko, an ancient coastal port on the Mediterranean, north of Haifa, to experience konafi the way it was meant to be.

Before we go further, it's helpful to distinguish between kataifi, the long, thin threads of dough used to make dozens of Arabic confections, and konafi, the specific pastry made by baking layers of kataifi sandwiched around a filling, then saturating the whole thing with flavored syrup.

Kataifi is referred to as "shredded phyllo dough" so often that you'd be forgiven for thinking it was true. But it is actually made from a thin batter of semolina and water. Originally it was drizzled by hand in individual strands onto a heated surface, but in modern times the process has become more automated. Now the batter is dispensed through tiny holes in an arm that cantilevers over a quickly revolving metal hot plate. The whole apparatus looks like a cross between a record player and spin art. Once the music stops, the threads of kataifi are gathered up into fluffy white wreaths.

Previous spread: The wizard of phyllo at Zalatimo's in Jerusalem's Old City. *This page:* Every ingredient is precious in the desserts at Kashash in Akko, including konafi *(top)*, cookies, and cheese pastry.

Kashash bakery makes its own kataifi, producing threads of dough so fine they look like they'd blow away in a light breeze. The kataifi is then mixed with melted butter and pressed into a rectangular pan, where it is layered with cheese and topped with more butter-soaked kataifi. The tray is placed on another spinning contraption over a burner so that the bottom of the konafi turns a uniform golden brown and the cheese oozes and melts. The konafi is flipped and the process is repeated on the other side. The crowning touch is a pour of saffron syrup and maybe a sprinkling of crushed pistachios.

One of the most common cheeses used in konafi throughout the Middle East is called *jibni Akkawi*—literally "cheese from Akko." It is a semi-firm cheese—most often made from cow's milk—that's brined in whey and then soaked before using. Osama is proud to report they still use Akko cheese at Kashash. (Fresh mozzarella is a credible substitute.)

A piece of fresh konafi sits on the table in front of us, still warm. We bite through the buttery crunch of the caramelized kataifi and reach the milky interior. The echo of salt in the melting cheese is the perfect counterpoint to the syrup-soaked pastry. The hype is real.

Kashash

AKKO | Where other bakeries use commodity ingredients, Kashash sources exotic nuts and spices and makes its own kataifi, the pastry threads that are essential to some of the most important desserts in the Arabic world, especially konafi. The local brined cheese from Akko called jibni Akkawi is the perfect foil for the rose-scented syrup that hydrates and sweetens the konafi after it's cooked.

Helman Bakery

JERUSALEM | Imagine a bakery that began as a brick factory in prewar Transylvania. When that business failed, the rabbi suggested repurposing the kilns: "Don't make bricks, make bread!" Communism forced the Helman family to leave Romania in 1958 for Israel, where they opened a new bakery in Jerusalem in 1965. Helman has made European Jewish specialties like cheesecakes, babkas, and poppy seed tarts ever since.

SAFFRON SYRUP   FROZEN KATAIFI   SUGAR   BUFFALO MOZZARELLA   UNSALTED BUTTER

Konafi

Serves 4

- 4   cups thawed frozen kataifi
- 3   tablespoons unsalted butter
- 2   tablespoons sugar
- 1   (8-ounce) ball fresh buffalo mozzarella, thinly sliced
- ½   cup Saffron Syrup

Put the kataifi in a bowl and comb through it with your fingers. Melt the butter in a stainless-steel or cast-iron skillet over low heat. Add the kataifi, spreading it out evenly and patting it down in the skillet. Sprinkle with the sugar and arrange the mozzarella slices on top. Cook until the cheese melts and the bottom is golden brown, 10 to 15 minutes. Remove from the heat. Invert onto a plate, drizzle with the Saffron Syrup, and cut into wedges.

Saffron Syrup

Makes about 2 cups

Even though orange food dye and carrots are commonly used for coloring today, we prefer the real thing. Combine 1 cup water, 2 cups sugar, and a large pinch of saffron threads in a small saucepan over medium heat. Cook, stirring constantly, until the mixture comes to a simmer and the sugar is completely dissolved. Remove from the heat and let cool to room temperature. Strain into a covered container. Refrigerated, the syrup will last for up to 6 months.

A. Measure 4 cups thawed frozen kataifi into a bowl. Comb through it with your fingers.

B. Melt the butter in a skillet, spread the kataifi evenly over it, and top with mozzarella slices.

C. When the cheese has melted and the bottom is golden, turn out onto a plate.

D. Drizzle spoonfuls of Saffron Syrup evenly over the pastry.

E. Close your eyes, grab a fork, take a bite, and imagine yourself in a bakery in ancient Akko.

HaMalabiya

TEL AVIV | The only thing new about the old-fashioned milk pudding called malabi is how fashionable it has become. Open late on a corner in the Carmel Market, HaMalabiya has put the hipster stamp of approval on custard. Step up to the bar and choose your syrup flavor and crunchy topping. Then kick back in the shade and take a break from the Tel Aviv sun with a game or two of backgammon.

Malabi

Serves 4

2 tablespoons sugar

2 teaspoons sachlab powder

¾ teaspoon agar agar powder

1 (13.5-ounce) can coconut milk

1 cup coconut cream

1 teaspoon orange blossom water

Concord grape jam, for topping

Cracked pistachios, for topping

A sweet, milk-based pudding traditionally thickened with cornstarch or rice flour and often topped with rose water syrup, malabi is an old-school street snack, perfect for cooling off in the blazing Mediterranean sun. It has recently become hip, appearing on restaurant dessert menus. There's even a dedicated malabi stall—**HaMalabiya**—on the edge of the Carmel Market in Tel Aviv. On Saturday afternoons, young people relax at the picnic tables, day-drinking, playing backgammon, and eating malabi with vanilla-cinnamon syrup and caramelized peanuts.

Our recipe uses coconut milk and coconut cream and is thickened with agar agar (a seaweed derivative), creating a vegan dessert that doubles as a kosher end to a meat meal. I love to add orchid root powder (also called sachlab) to our malabi. Sachlab was originally prized for its thickening power in addition to its heady flavor and aroma. There are plenty of cheaper, more effective thickeners, but nothing can replace sachlab's incomparable perfume. If you imagine "creamy" as a scent, you begin to get the idea. Notes of vanilla and mallow and fresh flowers add subtle but complex flavor to desserts, along with a luscious texture.

Malabi is a fairly neutral canvas for all kinds of toppings: flavored syrups, chopped nuts, or crushed cookies—they all make a good thing better. Here we use Concord grape jam and pistachios, but the combination possibilities are endless. Pomegranate syrup with a drop of rose water, orange syrup with shredded coconut, or a drizzle of honey and some salt-roasted peanuts all are great. For an interactive dessert, set out custard cups of plain malabi alongside dishes of toppings and let your guests go nuts. Ain't no party like a malabi party.

1. Whisk together the sugar, sachlab, and agar agar in a small bowl and set aside. Bring the coconut milk, coconut cream, and orange blossom water to a boil in a medium saucepan. When the mixture begins to boil, whisk in the sachlab mixture. Return to a boil and cook, whisking constantly until thickened, 2 to 3 minutes.

2. Remove from the heat and pour into a large serving dish or individual bowls. Let rest at room temperature until completely cooled and set, 20 to 30 minutes. Top with the jam and pistachios.

One of the holiest places on earth: The Church of the Holy Sepulchre in the Christian Quarter of Jerusalem's Old City is said to be the site of the tomb of Jesus.

Zalatimo

Serves 4 (makes two 10-inch pastries)

DOUGH

- 2 cups all-purpose flour
- ½ cup canola oil, plus more for oiling the counter and rolling pin
- 2 teaspoons kosher salt
- ½ cup water
- 2 tablespoons unsalted butter, melted

SYRUP

- ½ cup sugar
- ¼ cup honey
- ¼ cup water
- Zest and juice of 1 large lemon

ASSEMBLY

- 1½ cups ricotta cheese
- Melted butter, for brushing the dough
- Ground pistachios

Hidden behind the Church of the Holy Sepulchre (where Jesus is said to have been buried and resurrected) in the Old City of Jerusalem is **Zalatimo's** café, maybe less famous, but also known for delivering a religious experience. The basis for the café's signature treat is a phyllo-like dough that is rolled out by hand—wait for it—to order! It begins with a small round of dough that Hani Zalatimo flattens into a plate-size circle using a short, oiled rolling pin.

Then, with the nonchalance of a champion bullfighter, Mr. Zalatimo lifts the sheet of dough and twirls it just above the oiled stone counter. He rotates his right wrist around his left so that the dough unfurls like a sail, gathering air before he slaps it down on the oiled counter. He repeats this process a dozen times in a staccato rhythm, as the dough gets thinner and thinner and larger and larger. It's a technique more than 150 years in the making.

When the dough is paper-thin and the size of a movie poster, the edges are folded in to form a square. Then comes a sprinkling of crumbled sheep's milk cheese from Nablus (and maybe nuts, the only optional menu item). Finally, the corners are folded into the center like a child's paper fortune-teller (spoiler alert: The future is delicious).

When the pastry emerges from the oven, bubbled and golden, it is anointed with syrup and a dusting of confectioners' sugar and cut into quarters. The official name of the pastry is *mutabak*, which means "folded" in Arabic, but everyone calls it a Zalatimo, for obvious reasons. The café is partially underground, with a few tables, no decor, and one wall that is said to date back to the time of King Herod. It is also notoriously difficult to locate; to find it we had to maneuver through the Ethiopian monastery adjacent to the church. Perhaps it's only visible to true believers. Our version may have fewer flourishes, but it delivers a similar spiritual revelation.

Zalatimo's

JERUSALEM | Mr. Zalatimo's great-great-grandfather Mohammad Zalatimo opened the shop in 1860, not long after the Ottoman-decreed "status quo" fixed the custody of the Church of the Holy Sepulchre between the Greek, Armenian, and Roman Catholic churches.

1. **MAKE THE DOUGH:** Put the flour in the bowl of a stand mixer fitted with the dough hook, or use a large bowl and a hand mixer, and make a well in the center of the flour. Add the oil, salt, and water to the well. Mix for 5 minutes. Cover the bowl with plastic wrap and let relax at room temperature until smooth and elastic, 2 to 3 hours.

2. **MAKE THE SYRUP:** Combine the sugar, honey, water, and lemon zest and juice in a small saucepan over medium-high heat. Bring to a boil, whisking frequently to make sure the sugar is completely dissolved, then remove from the heat. Strain the syrup into a small bowl.

3. Preheat the oven to 425°F, with a rack in the lowest position. Brush two 10-inch ovenproof skillets with the melted butter and set aside.

4. Uncover the dough. Coat your work surface with canola oil. Turn out the dough, pat it into a long log shape, and cut it into 4 even pieces. Move 3 of the dough pieces to the side and cover them with a clean kitchen towel.

5. Using your hands, pat the first piece of dough into a rough circle. Oil your rolling pin and roll out the dough as thin as you can into a round shape, brushing the dough with a little oil as needed to keep it from sticking to the rolling pin.

6. Pick up the dough and lay it gently across one of the prepared skillets so that it hangs over the edges by about 2 inches on both sides. (You'll need those extra flaps to fold over the filling.) Roll out a second piece of dough and lay it across the skillet in the other direction. Spread the ricotta in the center of the dough. Fold the 4 flaps of dough over the

The heavenly pastry of ethereal flakiness at Zalatimo's. *Below:* A glimpse of the Old City.

ricotta one by one, brushing each piece with melted butter as you go. Roll out the remaining 2 pieces of dough and repeat the process in the second skillet with the remaining ricotta and more melted butter.

7. Put the skillets over medium heat and cook until the dough browns a little on the bottom, 5 to 8 minutes. Use a large spatula to flip the pastries, then transfer the skillets to the oven. Bake until golden and puffed, about 20 minutes. Invert the pastries onto plates and spoon half the syrup (about ½ cup) on top of each. Top with pistachios. Cut each pastry into four wedges and serve warm. Zalatimo, like pancakes, are best eaten as they're made.

A. Oil the counter, pat one piece of dough into a circle, and roll out.

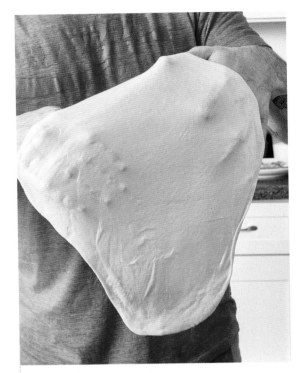

B. This is fun: Stretch the dough a bit with your fingers as you pick it up from the counter.

C. Gently lay the dough circle across a skillet, letting it hang over the edge by about 2 inches.

D. Lay a second piece of dough in the skillet in the opposite direction and spread the ricotta in the center.

E. Fold the flaps of dough in from all four sides, brushing each with melted butter as you go.

F. Brown the pastry's bottom, then flip and brown the top. Bake for 20 minutes. Spoon on the syrup.

G. Sprinkle lots of freshly ground pistachios over the top of the finished pastry.

H. Cut each pastry into four wedges and serve it up while it's still warm and flaky.

Yeasted Rugelach

Makes 32 cookies

DOUGH

- ⅔ cup sugar
- ¾ cup warm water
- 1 teaspoon active dry yeast
- ¼ cup canola oil
- 5 tablespoons labneh
- 1 teaspoon kosher salt
- 1 teaspoon vanilla extract
- 4 cups all-purpose flour

FILLING

- ¼ cup semisweet chocolate chips
- 2 tablespoons cocoa powder
- 4 tablespoons sugar
- 1 teaspoon kosher salt
- ⅓ cup heavy cream
- 3 tablespoons labneh
- 4 tablespoons almond butter
- 2 tablespoons unsalted butter, at room temperature

SUGAR SYRUP

- 1 cup sugar
- ½ cup water

Rugelach are a classic Ashkenazi Jewish cookie consisting of a triangle of dough rolled into a crescent shape around a sweet filling. They reached their pinnacle of fame in America, where cream cheese–enriched dough became the standard-bearer. But yeasted versions of rugelach are at least as old as their unleavened cousins and tend to be more common in Israel today. What is fascinating about this recipe is how it combines the Middle Eastern tradition of saturating pastries with sugar syrup with an Ashkenazi dough, producing a result that can truly only be called Israeli.

1. MAKE THE DOUGH: Whisk the sugar with the water until the sugar is completely dissolved, then pour into the bowl of a stand mixer fitted with the dough hook, or use a large bowl and a hand mixer. Stir in the yeast by hand and let stand until foamy, 5 to 10 minutes. Add the oil, labneh, salt, and vanilla. Mix to combine, then add the flour. Mix on low speed until the dough comes together and is smooth, 2 to 3 minutes. Cover the bowl and set aside at room temperature until it doubles in volume, about 1 hour.

2. MAKE THE FILLING: Mix together the chocolate chips, cocoa, sugar, salt, cream, labneh, almond butter, and butter in a large bowl.

3. ASSEMBLE THE RUGELACH: Preheat the oven to 375°F and position racks in the top and bottom thirds. Line two baking sheets with parchment paper. Divide the dough into 2 equal pieces and place on a lightly floured surface. Roll both pieces into large rectangles about ⅛ inch thick. Spread both rectangles with the filling.

4. For both log- and crescent-shaped rolls, carefully lift one rectangle of dough and place it on top of the other so you have two layers of dough and two layers of filling.

5. For log-shaped rolls, beginning at one long end, tightly roll up the dough into a skinny log and cut it into 16 slices, about 1 inch thick.

6. For crescent-shaped rolls, use a sharp knife to cut the layered dough into 16 triangles. Starting with the widest edge, roll each triangle into a coil.

7. Arrange the rolls on the prepared baking sheets and let rise at room temperature for 1 hour. Bake until light brown, 8 to 10 minutes, rotating at the halfway point from top to bottom and back to front.

8. MEANWHILE, MAKE THE SYRUP: Combine the sugar and water in a small saucepan over medium heat. Stir every few minutes until the sugar is dissolved. Remove from the heat.

9. Pour the syrup over the rugelach when they come out of the oven.

10. Let the rugelach cool on a wire rack before serving. They will keep for 2 days at room temperature.

Hamantaschen

Makes about 3 dozen cookies

16 tablespoons (2 sticks) unsalted butter, at room temperature

1 cup granulated sugar

½ cup light brown sugar

1 large egg

3 tablespoons whole milk

1 teaspoon vanilla extract

¼ teaspoon maple extract (optional)

3 cups all-purpose flour

1½ teaspoons baking powder

½ teaspoon kosher salt

1 (12-ounce) jar apricot preserves

These jam-filled cookies are supposed to resemble the tricornered hat of Haman, one of the great villains in Jewish history. The springtime holiday of Purim celebrates the deliverance of the Jews of Persia from certain doom thanks to the bravery of the Jewish Queen Esther and her cousin Mordecai.

Purim is one of the most festive holidays on the Jewish calendar, involving dressing up in costumes, giving gifts to friends and the poor, and drinking until you can't tell the difference between Haman and Mordecai. For those below the drinking age, making hamantaschen is a fun way to get in on the action. This is Steve's mother's recipe, and we love to make them with our kids. Sally and Leo Cook (below) are fearless bakers.

1. Beat together the butter, both sugars, the egg, milk, vanilla, and maple extract (if using) in the bowl of a stand mixer fitted with the paddle attachment, or use a large bowl and a hand mixer. Add the flour, baking powder, and salt and beat until fully incorporated. Form the dough into a ball, wrap in wax paper, and refrigerate for at least 4 hours or up to overnight.

2. Preheat the oven to 375°F and position racks in the top and bottom thirds. Line two baking sheets with parchment paper. Roll the dough out on a floured surface to ⅛ inch thick. Use the rim of a juice glass or cup to cut out 3-inch circles. Put a teaspoon of the preserves in each circle, then fold in the edges to form a triangle, pinching at the corners to keep the filling in, but leaving the center filling slightly exposed. Arrange on the prepared baking sheets and bake until lightly browned, 8 to 10 minutes, rotating at the halfway point from top to bottom and back to front.

3. Let the hamantaschen cool on a wire rack. They will keep at room temperature for 2 days.

Coconut Almond Basboosa

Makes one 10-inch cake

Canola oil, for the
pan

½ cup almonds,
toasted

1¼ cups semolina
flour

1½ cups granulated
sugar

2½ tablespoons
almond paste

¾ cup coconut
milk, at room
temperature

1 tablespoon
coconut extract

½ cup almond flour

1 teaspoon baking
soda

½ teaspoon baking
powder

¼ teaspoon kosher
salt

8 tablespoons
(1 stick) unsalted
butter, melted
and slightly
cooled

2 large eggs,
at room
temperature

¼ cup water

Confectioners'
sugar, for
dusting

In the realm of baked goods, basboosa is the best of both worlds: a cake with a toothsome semolina crumb that also stays incredibly moist from its saturation with flavored simple syrup.

Almond and coconut are classic basboosa ingredients. Our recipe goes for broke with the almonds, using four forms of the nut: whole almonds, almond paste, almond extract, and almond flour.

1. Preheat the oven to 350°F. Coat the bottom of a 10-inch round cake pan or springform pan with oil, line with parchment paper, and then oil again. Combine the toasted almonds and semolina in a food processor and grind into a fine meal. Transfer to a bowl and set aside. Combine 1 cup of the granulated sugar and the almond paste in the food processor and grind until the almond paste is completely incorporated into the sugar. Set aside. Mix together the coconut milk and coconut extract in a small bowl.

2. Beat together the almond flour, baking soda, baking powder, salt, the almond-semolina mixture, and the sugar–almond paste mixture in the bowl of a stand mixer fitted with the paddle attachment, or in a large bowl using a hand mixer. With the mixer on low speed, stream in the melted butter and mix until it is completely incorporated. Add the eggs, one at a time, making sure each one is completely incorporated before adding the next. Add the coconut milk mixture a little at a time, mixing between each addition until it is fully incorporated into the batter.

3. Pour the batter into the prepared pan. Bake for 35 minutes, rotating back to front at the halfway point, until a cake tester inserted into the center comes out clean.

4. While the cake bakes, bring the remaining ½ cup sugar and the water to a boil in a small saucepan, whisking frequently to make sure the sugar is completely dissolved. Remove from the heat and let the syrup cool slightly.

5. When the cake is done baking, remove from the oven, pour ¼ to ½ cup of the syrup over the top, and let cool on a wire rack. Remove the cake from the pan and dust with confectioners' sugar before serving.

Mike Ran's Mom's Coffee Cake

Makes one (10-inch) cake

BATTER

- 3 cups all-purpose flour
- 2 teaspoons baking powder
- 1 teaspoon baking soda
- 1 teaspoon kosher salt
- 16 tablespoons (2 sticks) unsalted butter, at room temperature, plus more for the pan
- 1½ cups granulated sugar
- 3 large eggs
- 1 (16-ounce) container labneh or sour cream

TOPPING

- ⅔ cup packed brown sugar
- ½ cup granulated sugar
- 2 teaspoons ground cinnamon
- 2 teaspoons vanilla extract
- 1 cup semisweet chocolate chips

The Jewish food canon is filled with dishes designed to be ready to eat on Shabbat without further cooking. Our American-Jewish answer to Saturday morning breakfast when I was growing up was the Entenmann's coffee cake. I remember going to the factory outlet store with my mother and stocking up on Butter French Crumb Cake, Raspberry Danish Twist, and Crumb Topped Donuts. Mike Ran worked with us in the kitchens at Zahav and Rooster Soup Company. He is a nice Jewish boy from Detroit, and if his mom's coffee cake recipe is any indication, he was raised right.

Serve with Turkish Coffee *(opposite)*.

1. MAKE THE BATTER: Preheat the oven to 375°F. Butter a 10-inch round cake pan or springform pan. Whisk together the flour, baking powder, baking soda, and salt in a large bowl. Beat the butter and granulated sugar in the bowl of a stand mixer fitted with the paddle attachment, or use a large bowl and a hand mixer. Add the eggs, one at a time, beating after each addition. Gradually add the dry ingredients, beating between additions, and finally beat in the labneh. Pour half the batter into the prepared pan and spread it evenly.

2. MAKE THE TOPPING: Mix together the brown sugar, granulated sugar, cinnamon, vanilla, and chocolate chips in a medium bowl.

3. Spread half the topping over the batter in the pan. Pour in the rest of the batter, smooth the top, and spread with the rest of the topping in an even layer. Bake until a tester comes out clean when inserted into the center of the cake, 45 minutes to 1 hour. Let rest for at least 10 minutes. Remove the cake from the pan and let cool on a wire rack.

Turkish Coffee

Makes 1 serving

Israel has always had a strong coffee culture, influenced by the European roots of the early pioneers as well as by the standards of Arabic hospitality. Consequently, Israelis spend a lot of time drinking coffee in cafés and not so much taking coffee to go. And whether you are negotiating a business transaction or dropping in on a friend for a social call, there's a good chance you will be offered coffee.

Turkish coffee (aka Arabic coffee, aka Israeli coffee) uses perhaps the simplest brewing method around. It requires only a heat source and a small, long-handled pot called a finjan in Israel, or an ibrik in Turkey (you can use a saucepan). But the difference between good and bad Turkish coffee lies in a few small details. The sugar must be added at the beginning of the process. The grind of the coffee must be just right. The water must be brought up to a bare simmer very slowly. The coffee must be stirred at the right time. And there must be enough headroom for the coffee to expand and create a proper layer of foam.

This careful, exacting ritual serves two purposes. First, it ensures a cup of coffee that is worth drinking. But, just as important, it also represents the care with which the host provides hospitality to a guest.

Combine 1 tablespoon Turkish coffee, 1 cup water, and 1 teaspoon sugar in a Turkish coffee pot or small saucepan. Heat until it just starts to bubble, stirring a few times, then immediately remove from the stove. Be careful not to let the coffee come to a boil (which would make it taste burnt). Pour into an espresso cup and serve with a small glass of water on the side. Allow the grounds to settle for about 30 seconds before drinking.

Okan Yazici, Zahav

PHILADELPHIA | A native of Istanbul, Okan was a serious soccer player before an injury derailed his professional ambitions. He joined Zahav as a busser after we opened in 2008, and, quickly progressing through virtually every job in the restaurant, he became general manager in 2015. Okan is the embodiment of hospitality, and no one is more responsible for Zahav's success!

Easy Ma'amoul Cookies

Makes about 32 cookies

13 tablespoons plus 1 teaspoon (1⅓ sticks) unsalted butter, at room temperature

2½ cups bread flour

6 tablespoons semolina flour

¾ cup sugar

1½ teaspoons baking powder

⅓ cup whole milk

1 teaspoon orange blossom water

½ teaspoon vanilla extract

Jam or fruit preserves

Confectioners' sugar, for dusting

Ma'amoul are traditional Arabic shortbread cookies made with semolina and stuffed with a paste of nuts or dried fruit. Making ma'amoul is a labor-intensive process involving an intricately decorated wooden mold that is used to encase the filling inside the dough. As a result, ma'amoul have historically been reserved for a special-occasion treat, most often associated with Eid al-Fitr, the three-day celebration immediately following Ramadan, the Muslim month of fasting. In a similar vein, Levantine Christians eat ma'amoul on Easter, a reward for enduring the deprivations of Lent.

Levantine Jewish communities in Syria, Egypt, and Lebanon were also ma'amoul enthusiasts and brought them to Israel, where they remain popular. They are most common during Purim, with a traditional filling of seeds and nuts, and on Rosh Hashanah and Hanukkah, when they are stuffed with dates.

We wanted a simple ma'amoul. This recipe trades the stuffed version for a thumbprint-style cookie that is the perfect treat to accompany a cup of Turkish coffee *(page 343)*.

1. Preheat the oven to 350°F and position racks in the top and bottom thirds. Line two baking sheets with parchment paper. Beat the butter in the bowl of a stand mixer fitted with the paddle attachment, or use a large bowl and a hand mixer, until it is very smooth. Combine the bread flour, semolina, sugar, and baking powder in a bowl. Combine the milk, orange blossom water, and vanilla in another bowl. Alternate adding the dry and wet mixtures to the butter, mixing well between each addition, until everything is incorporated.

2. Roll tablespoon-size pieces of the dough into balls and place them on the prepared baking sheets, about 1 inch apart. Make an indentation with your thumb in the center of each piece of dough and fill it with jam or preserves. Bake until puffed and light brown on the bottom, 8 to 10 minutes, rotating the baking sheets at the halfway point from top to bottom and back to front. Remove from the oven and let cool on a wire rack. Ma'amoul will keep at room temperature in a covered container for 1 week. Dust with confectioners' sugar before serving.

Labneh Tart

Makes one 9-inch tart

CRUST

- 10 whole graham crackers
- 6 tablespoons unsalted butter, at room temperature
- ¼ cup granulated sugar
- Pinch of kosher salt

FILLING

- 1 (14-ounce) can sweetened condensed milk
- ⅓ cup lemon juice
- ¼ cup granulated sugar
- ½ cup confectioners' sugar
- 1 teaspoon grated orange zest
- ⅛ teaspoon kosher salt
- 1 (16-ounce) container labneh

Fresh raspberries or sliced strawberries, for topping

New York cheesecake meets Israel in this recipe that combines a Western graham cracker crust with a labneh-based filling from the Middle East. This is ridiculously simple to put together—just leave enough time for the filling to set up in the refrigerator. A graham cracker crust delivers the best bang for the buck in terms of the effort required (minimal) versus the result (awesome)—a far better ratio than a traditional piecrust or tart shell, and it's foolproof as well. Tangy labneh makes for a lighter filling than cream cheese, so feel free to eat two slices.

1. MAKE THE CRUST: Put the graham crackers in a food processor and process until finely ground; you should have about 1½ cups crumbs. Add the butter, granulated sugar, and salt and process until the butter is fully incorporated and the mixture resembles wet sand. Press into the bottom and up the side of a 9-inch round tart pan. Cover and refrigerate for at least 2 hours or overnight.

2. MAKE THE FILLING: Combine the condensed milk, lemon juice, both sugars, the orange zest, and salt in the bowl of a stand mixer fitted with the paddle attachment, or use a large bowl and a hand mixer. Mix on medium speed until smooth, then add the labneh and continue mixing just until combined (too much mixing will cause the labneh to break, preventing the tart from setting). Pour into the prepared crust, cover, and refrigerate for at least 8 hours or up to overnight. Serve topped with fresh berries.

Fried Challah Sufganiyot

Makes about 24 donuts

DONUTS

- ½ cup sugar
- 1 packet active dry yeast
- 1 cup warm water
- 3¾ cups all-purpose flour
- 1 teaspoon kosher salt
- 1 tablespoon plus 2 teaspoons olive oil
- 3 tablespoons canola oil, plus more for frying
- ½ cup egg yolks (about 6 large yolks)
- ⅔ cup butter, at room temperature
- 2 cups quince (or other fruit) jam

ROSE PETAL SUGAR

- 1 cup sugar
- ½ cup crushed dried rose petals

The Jewish holiday of Hanukkah commemorates the successful Jewish revolt against the provincial Greek government of Judea during the time of the Second Temple (between 530 BCE and 70 CE, if you're curious). Led by the Maccabees, the Jews reclaimed the desecrated temple, but they found only one day's worth of purified oil to light the menorah, which was required to burn continuously. Miraculously, the oil lasted for eight days, enough time for a fresh supply to arrive.

During the eight days of Hanukkah, we celebrate that miracle by eating foods fried in oil, rivaling Halloween for best gratuitous reason to eat junk food—holiday division. Latkes steal most of the Hanukkah spotlight, but sufganiyot—yeast-raised, jelly-filled donuts—are ever popular. Throughout Israel, bakeries turn into donut factories, producing tray after tray of plump, light, and golden brown beauties. We've found that eggy challah dough, enriched with butter and sugar, makes a great donut batter that's easy to work with. Instead of rolling out the dough and punching out rings as with traditional yeast donuts, we use an ice cream scoop to form and dispense the sufganiyot into the oil.

We love the exotic and festive combination of quince jam and rose petal sugar, but feel free to substitute any jam and sugar combination. May we suggest our *Federal Donuts* cookbook for inspiration?

1. MAKE THE DONUTS: Combine the sugar, yeast, and water in the bowl of a stand mixer fitted with the dough hook. Let stand until foamy, about 5 minutes. Add the flour, salt, olive oil, canola oil, and egg yolks. Mix on low speed until the dough comes together and begins to pull away from the sides of the bowl, about 1 minute.

2. Gradually mix in the butter, mixing for another minute. Scrape down the side of the bowl and continue mixing for 2 more minutes. Cover the bowl and let the dough rise at room temperature until it has quadrupled in volume, about 4 hours.

3. Fill a large pot with a generous 2 inches of canola oil. Heat over medium heat until the oil registers 350°F on a candy thermometer. Line a baking sheet with paper towels.

4. Use an ice cream scoop to drop balls of dough into the hot oil, adjusting the heat as necessary to maintain the oil temperature. Fry the donuts in batches until golden, 4 to 6 minutes. Remove from the pot with a slotted spoon to drain on the prepared baking sheet. Let cool slightly.

5. MAKE THE ROSE PETAL SUGAR: Combine the sugar and crushed rose petals in a shallow bowl.

6. Poke a hole in each donut with the tip of a paring knife. Spoon the jam into a large resealable plastic bag, press out the air, and twist the top until the bag feels tight. Snip off a corner of the bag and squeeze the jam into each donut until a bit oozes out. Roll the filled donuts in the rose petal sugar. Serve warm.

Pistachio Cake

Makes one 10-inch cake

CAKE

- 3 tablespoons cornstarch
- ½ cup pistachios
- ¼ cup almond flour
- 4 sticks (1 pound) unsalted butter, at room temperature
- ¼ cup sugar
- ⅓ cup pistachio paste
- 5 large egg whites plus 3 large eggs

PISTACHIO SUGAR

- 2 tablespoons ground pistachios
- 2 tablespoons sugar

Sliced hulled strawberries, for topping (optional)

I've loved frangipane since my days in culinary school. There's some kind of magic in the way this confection of almond paste, butter, sugar, and eggs bakes up into something that's half cake, half custard.

Pistachios have been part of the diet in what is now Israel for thousands of years, and they are an essential component of desserts throughout the Middle East. So it seemed only natural to substitute them for the almonds in this frangipane-inspired recipe. Pistachios also happen to be my personal favorite nut. I love everything about them: their sweet, vegetal flavor; their gorgeous green color; and their fun-to-eat, waxy texture. And this dessert is gluten-free! A growing number of our restaurant guests follow a gluten-free diet, and I love being able to end their meals with a simple, delicious dessert without compromise.

Frangipane is frequently baked in a traditional pastry shell, but the extra egg whites in this recipe provide enough structure for it to stand on its own. This cake is great served with fresh fruit, but you can also pour the batter over poached or roasted fruit in the bottom of the pan.

1. MAKE THE CAKE: Grind the cornstarch and pistachios in a food processor until the mixture resembles coarsely ground flour. Combine with the almond flour in a bowl.

2. Combine the butter, sugar, and pistachio paste in the bowl of a stand mixer fitted with the paddle attachment, or use a large bowl and a hand mixer, and beat until light and fluffy. Gradually add the egg whites and eggs, beating after each addition and scraping down the side of the bowl as needed. Add the pistachio-flour mixture and beat until incorporated. Cover and refrigerate for at least 1 hour or up to overnight.

3. Preheat the oven to 325°F. Coat a 10-inch cake pan with cooking spray, line the bottom with parchment paper, then spray it again. Pour in the batter and smooth the top. Bake until a cake tester comes out clean, about 30 minutes. Remove the cake from the pan and let cool on a wire rack. The cake will keep, covered, at room temperature for up to 2 days.

4. MAKE THE PISTACHIO SUGAR: Mix together the ground pistachios and sugar in a small bowl.

5. Before serving, sprinkle the pistachio sugar on the cake. Top with sliced strawberries, if you like.

Sesame Brittle

Makes sixty-four 1-inch pieces

Canola oil, for the baking dish
1 cup sesame seeds
¼ cup honey
¼ cup sugar
Pinch of kosher salt
1 tablespoon tehina

This is our version of the individually wrapped miniature bricks of sesame candy that are ubiquitous in Israel. We always keep a jar of them on the counter at Dizengoff. This recipe is a great introduction to candy-making. We add a little tehina to the mix, which is nontraditional but reinforces the sesame flavor and helps keep the candies tender when they harden.

1. Coat an 8-inch-square baking dish lightly with oil. Combine the sesame seeds, honey, sugar, and salt in a saucepan. Bring to a boil over medium-high heat and cook for 2 minutes, stirring vigorously. Stir in the tehina, return the mixture to a boil, and cook for 1½ to 2 more minutes, or until thickened. Stir vigorously and scrape the mixture into the prepared baking dish, using the back of a spoon to spread it into an even layer.

2. Let cool slightly, then slide the brittle onto a board and cut it into 1-inch cubes. Enjoy as is (it will be a bit chewy), or let sit at room temperature until completely hardened, about 1 hour. The brittle will keep in a covered container at room temperature for 2 weeks.

CHAPTER 15

Drinks & Cold Treats

"Seltzer became so popular among our people it was called 'Jewish Champagne.'"

One hot summer's day on the Lower East Side, a Jewish man fainted from the heat. A doctor happened to be walking by and rushed over to examine him. "Someone bring him a glass of water!" he cried. The man opened his eyes and raised his head off the pavement. "Make it seltzer," he moaned.

The great-grandfather of Steve's wife, Shira, moved to Pittsburgh near the turn of the century, lured by a job as a machinist for the Westinghouse Electric Corporation. Eventually he started Burke Bottling Company, a seltzer business that delivered heavy glass siphon bottles to the doorsteps of his (mostly Jewish) customers. At some point, Burke was approached by representatives of a new soft drink brand that was gearing up to take on Coca-Cola, asking if he would become the exclusive Pittsburgh bottler of the new beverage. He turned them down, saying, "No one will ever touch Coca-Cola." He was right. Sort of. Pepsi would always come in second. Burke stuck with seltzer, a drink with proven demand.

Jews and seltzer are inextricably linked. A non-Jewish friend was a frequent guest at my house for Shabbat dinner, and, over time, he memorized the rituals of the meal: First there was the Kiddush, the blessing over the wine, followed by the Motzi, the blessing over the bread. And finally, he said, it was time for the seltzer.

Benny Briga, Café Levinsky 41

TEL AVIV | For modern tastes, a visit to Benny Briga's Café Levinsky 41 is in order. Benny is a former cook turned mad scientist, whose herb-and-fruit-and-seltzer creations *(previous spread)* infuse gazoz, as Israelis call it, with new vitality and relevance. The backlit shelves at his tiny stall in Levinsky Market are filled with glass bottles and jars full of colorful elixirs and fruits preserved in syrup. A pickup truck permanently parked out front is fitted with benches that share space with overflowing pots of herbs. It is part apothecary, part bohemian café.

With shoulder-length salt-and-pepper hair and a trim goatee, Benny resembles a young wizard just beginning to fully understand his powers. No two of his drinks are alike, and there is no menu. Benny's kind, piercing eyes size you up as he assembles your drink in a tall plastic cup. Instead of using artificial syrups, he concocts his own combinations that showcase the incredible bounty of Israel.

He's gathered a multitude of intoxicating ingredients: apricots, guava, figs, limes, and goji berries, combined with rosemary, lavender, hyssop, sage, and rose geranium. And then there's juniper, vanilla, star anise, cinnamon, and ginger. These potions are topped off with fresh seltzer from the tap, just like the first gazoz a century ago.

Avihai Tsabari

TEL AVIV | I met Avihai on the film shoot for *In Search of Israeli Cuisine*, where director Roger Sherman hired him as guide and fixer. We became instant friends and quickly discovered that he had been my mom's student in high school (Israel is a very small country).

My mom remembered him as lazy and uninterested, a far cry from Avihai today—the founder and creative force behind Via Sabra, one of Israel's leading tour companies. After a brief but distinguished military career, Avihai worked in the restaurant industry, then undertook the rigorous study required to become a guide.

The son of a Yemenite father and Tunisian mother, Avihai is fully engaged in the Israeli obsession of searching the country for the very best version of any particular dish. He utilizes those skills for Via Sabra's clients, and helped us every step of the way as we ate and debated our way through Israel for this book.

Many Jewish immigrants had been seltzer manufacturers in Europe, so it was natural for them to take up the trade in America. Seltzer—nicknamed "two cents plain"—was the cheapest drink at the soda counters that sprouted up all over New York just as Jewish immigrants were arriving in droves. And it does go well with a pastrami sandwich.

But it's interesting to note that this exact habit developed in Israel around the same time. The word *seltzer* derives from the German town of Niederseltsers, near Frankfurt. During the sixteenth century, the town began producing naturally carbonated tonic water reputed to have therapeutic benefits. An Englishman first made soda water in the late eighteenth century as an inexpensive alternative to naturally carbonated mineral spring waters. A few years later, a Swiss watchmaker named Schweppe commercialized the process. And then, in 1829, two Frenchmen invented the forerunner of the siphon, which allowed the user to dispense a portion of the carbonated water in the bottle while maintaining pressure on what remained. (Even 200 years ago people despised flat soda.)

The French called theirs *eau gazeuse* ("gassed water"), which morphed into *gazoz* when it made its way to the Ottoman Empire. To this day, Turkey's flavored gazoz are a beloved, though waning, part of the country's soft drink culture. The Ottomans brought gazoz to Palestine at the turn of the twentieth century—about the same time that the New Yorkers developed a taste for it. As in New York, Jewish settlers enthusiastically embraced the beverage. Pushcarts and kiosks were the Israeli version of American soda fountains, dispensing carbonated water that was sometimes flavored with sweetened fruit syrup concentrate. But Israeli gazoz had a much longer life. After Independence, Israel had no hard currency to import consumer products like Coke and few willing trading partners.

Over time, though, gazoz was all but swallowed up by the bottled soft drink industry. Some vestiges still remain, like at **Itzik and Ruti** on Shenkin Street in Tel Aviv, where the window counter is lined with jewel-toned syrups that remind Israelis of a certain age of childhood treats. This *gazoz shel paam* ("soda of then") appeals to a nostalgia for the formative years of a country where deprivation and ingenuity were cornerstones of its developing culture. These feelings remain, despite the fact that most syrups are neon-colored, cloying, and artificially flavored.

Juice Sellers

Having fresh-squeezed juice at your fingertips is one of life's affordable luxuries and a defining feature of Israeli street life. On a hot day, for a few shekels, you can treat yourself to a glass of orange or grapefruit juice that is alive with the pure essence of the fruit. We're particularly partial to pomegranate juice.

WATERMELON JUICE   TURMERIC-LIME SYRUP   MINT   ICE CUBES

POMEGRANATE JUICE   LIME   CUCUMBER   DILL FRONDS   SELTZER

Brian Kane, Abe Fisher

PHILADELPHIA | After a stint waiting tables at some of Chicago's temples of gastronomy, Brian returned to his hometown as a server at Zahav. He was quickly promoted to manager and beverage director, and he assembled the largest Israeli wine list in the country.

In 2014 Brian became the general manager of our Abe Fisher, where he put together an award-winning beverage program that complements the restaurant's take on European Jewish cuisine. When he is not thinking about wine, cocktails, or amaro, Brian's listening to live music (unless he's playing it as a guitarist in a Joan Jett cover band).

Fruit Sodas

You don't need a pushcart or a kiosk to make homemade sodas that are tastier than their bottled counterparts. The basic formula is simple: a syrup made of fruit juice, sugar, and citrus, embellished with herbs, spices, and other aromatics, and crowned with Jewish Champagne. Here are but a few of the blended fruit syrups we serve at our restaurants. *L'chaim!*

For each drink, fill a glass with ice. Pour in 2 ounces of syrup and top off with seltzer. Stir well and add a jaunty slice of citrus or cucumber, or a sprig of herbs. All fruit syrups will keep, refrigerated, for up to 1 month.

Pomegranate-Mint Syrup

Makes about 3½ cups

1	**cup pomegranate juice**
1	**cup lemon juice**
1½	**cups sugar**
1	**cup water**
1⅓	**cups chopped fresh mint**

Combine the pomegranate juice, lemon juice, sugar, and water in a medium saucepan and bring to a simmer over low heat, stirring frequently. Remove from the heat and add the mint. Let steep for 1 hour at room temperature, or until the syrup is completely cooled. Strain through a fine-mesh sieve into a jar.

Goldie Turmeric-Lime Syrup

Makes about 2½ cups

1 cup sugar
1¼ cups water
¼ cup lemon juice
½ teaspoon kosher salt
Grated zest of 1 lime
2 (2½-inch) pieces fresh turmeric, peeled and cut into chunks
1 cup lime juice

Combine the sugar and water in a small saucepan and bring to a rolling boil for 3 minutes, stirring to dissolve the sugar. Remove from the heat and let cool to room temperature. Pour the cooled syrup into a blender, along with the lemon juice, salt, lime zest, and turmeric. Puree until the turmeric is completely incorporated. Transfer to a jar, cover, and refrigerate overnight. The next day, add the lime juice. Shake well before mixing with seltzer.

Tarragon-Grapefruit Syrup

Makes about 2¼ cups

¾ cup grated grapefruit zest (from 4 to 5 large grapefruit)
1 cup grapefruit juice
¼ cup lemon juice
1 cup sugar
7 star anise pods, toasted
1 tablespoon fennel seeds, toasted
1 cup water
¾ cup chopped fresh tarragon

Combine the grapefruit zest and juice, lemon juice, sugar, star anise, fennel seeds, and water in a pot and bring to a simmer over low heat, stirring frequently. Remove from the heat, add the tarragon, and let steep at room temperature until completely cooled. Strain through a fine-mesh sieve into a jar.

Celery-Parsley-Dill Syrup

Makes about 2½ cups

CELERY WATER

1	**bunch celery, thoroughly washed, base cut off and discarded**
1¼	**cups water**

1	**cup lemon juice**
1	**cup sugar**
1	**cup chopped fresh parsley**
½	**cup chopped fresh dill**
¼	**teaspoon kosher salt**

1. MAKE THE CELERY WATER: Coarsely chop the celery and put in a blender with the water. Blend until smooth, then strain through a fine-mesh sieve into a measuring cup (you should have about 1¾ cups).

2. Pour the celery water back into the blender and add all the remaining ingredients. Blend until smooth and uniform in color, then strain through a fine-mesh sieve into a jar.

Watermelon-Lime Syrup

Makes about 3 cups

2	**cups watermelon juice**
1	**cup lime juice**
1½	**cups sugar**
1	**vanilla bean, split lengthwise**

Combine all the ingredients in a medium saucepan and bring to a simmer over low heat, stirring frequently. Remove from the heat and let cool to room temperature. Strain through a fine-mesh sieve into a jar.

Tehina Shakes

Makes 4 servings

½ cup tehina

½ cup sugar

½ teaspoon kosher salt

3 cups plain unsweetened almond milk, plus more as needed

¼ cup flavored syrup of your choice *(recipes follow)*, **plus more as needed**

Coconut Whip or Halva *(recipes follow)*, **or chopped chocolate and fresh mint, for topping**

When we conceived **Goldie Falafel**, instead of thinking of falafel as an ethnic specialty, we wanted to present it as a vegan alternative to saturated-fat-laden hamburgers, but still wrapped in the flag of the great American fast-food joint. Falafel and French fries—which are often stuffed into pita along with the falafel—were the easy part, since both are naturally vegan and fundamentally delicious.

But what about the milkshakes? How would we replace the sweet, rich, and creamy milkfat with something equally decadent, satisfying—and dairy-free? Fortunately, when the fast-food gods close a door, they open a window.

We've said it before: There are very few culinary problems that tehina can't solve. It's mostly fat, it's vegan, and it has a delicious (if forward) flavor that is great in sweet applications (*see also: Halva, page 363*). Mixed with sugar and a combination of soy and almond or coconut milks and run through an expensive milkshake machine, it yields something that could be (and often is) mistaken for a milkshake. From the opening day of Goldie on April 1, 2017, tehina shakes were a runaway hit, perhaps surpassing the falafel itself in popularity.

No milkshake machine? No problem. Caitlin McMillan, our partner and the chef who developed all of Goldie's recipes, including the tehina shakes, has adapted our process for ice cube trays and a blender.

1. Combine the tehina, sugar, salt, and almond milk in a blender. Process until smooth. Pour the mixture into ice cube trays (you'll need three standard-size trays) and freeze overnight.

2. The next day, pop the tehina ice cubes out of the trays into the blender. Pour in a little more almond milk to get the blender started and blend just until the ice cubes are completely broken down and the mixture thickens. Add the flavored syrup and blend for a few more seconds. Taste and add a bit more syrup if you like.

3. Pour the milkshake into glasses and serve immediately, topped with Coconut Whip or Halva, or with chopped chocolate and fresh mint.

Turkish Coffee with
Hazelnut Halva

Coconut Whip

Mint Chocolate Chip

A.

B.

Coconut Syrup

Makes 1½ to 2 cups

- ¾ cup unsweetened coconut flakes
- 1 (13.5-ounce) can coconut milk
- ¾ cup sugar
- ½ teaspoon kosher salt
- 1 teaspoon coconut extract
- 1 teaspoon rose water

1. Place a small skillet over medium heat and toast the coconut flakes, tossing frequently, just until they turn golden brown in spots. Remove from the heat and let cool.

2. Combine the coconut milk, sugar, salt, and coconut flakes in a medium saucepan over medium-high heat. Bring the mixture to a boil, then remove the pan from the heat, cover, and let steep overnight, refrigerated.

3. The next day, strain the syrup through a fine-mesh sieve into a jar and stir in the coconut extract and rose water. The syrup will keep, refrigerated, for up to 2 weeks.

Coconut Whip

Makes about 2 cups

- ¼ cup confectioners' sugar
- 1 teaspoon rose water
- ⅛ teaspoon salt
- 1 (13.5-ounce) can coconut milk, refrigerated overnight

Whisk together the confectioners' sugar, rose water, and salt in a large bowl. Gradually add the coconut milk, whisking constantly until soft peaks form. Top each shake with a generous dollop.

Turkish Coffee Syrup

Makes 1½ to 2 cups

- 2 cups water
- 6 tablespoons Turkish coffee
- 6 tablespoons regular ground coffee
- 6 tablespoons sugar
- ¾ teaspoon ground cardamom
- ¼ teaspoon kosher salt

Combine all the ingredients in a medium saucepan over medium-high heat. Bring to a boil, remove the pan from the heat, and let steep for 30 minutes. Place a coffee filter inside a fine-mesh sieve and set it over a jar. Strain the syrup into the jar. The syrup will keep, refrigerated, for up to 1 month.

C.

D.

Halva

Makes one 8-inch square pan

2¼ cups sugar
½ cup water
2¼ cups tehina
2 cups hazelnuts, toasted and chopped (optional)

1. Line the bottom and sides of an 8-inch square baking dish with parchment paper. Combine the sugar and water in a saucepan and heat to 240°F on a candy thermometer, whisking frequently. Meanwhile, place the tehina and hazelnuts, if using, in the bowl of a stand mixer fitted with the paddle attachment and beat until fully incorporated.

2. Carefully stream the sugar syrup into the tehina mixture with the mixer running on medium speed. Beat just until the syrup is incorporated and the mixture begins to pull away from the side of the bowl, no more than 1 minute. (You want a fudge-like consistency; if you mix too long, it will get crumbly.)

3. Working quickly, scrape the mixture into the prepared dish and press it out evenly. Let cool completely at room temperature, then cut into squares. Store in a covered container at room temperature for 1 week. Crumble a square of halva on top of each shake.

Mint Syrup

Makes 1½ to 2 cups

½ cup plus 6 tablespoons sugar
½ teaspoon plus ⅛ teaspoon kosher salt
1 cup plus 2 tablespoons water
¼ cup plus 1½ tablespoons packed fresh mint, plus more for topping
½ teaspoon mint extract
2½ teaspoons lemon juice
Your favorite chocolate bar

1. Combine the sugar, salt, water, and ¼ cup of the mint in a medium saucepan over medium-high heat. Bring the mixture to a boil, then remove from the heat and let steep until it has cooled to room temperature.

2. Strain the syrup through a fine-mesh sieve into a blender or food processor. Add the remaining 1½ tablespoons mint and process until it is incorporated into the syrup.

3. Pour the syrup into a jar and stir in the mint extract and lemon juice. The syrup will keep, refrigerated, for up to 1 month.

4. Scatter shards of chocolate and torn mint leaves on top of each shake.

Our ice-pop taste testers at work *(from left):* Lucas Solomonov; Eva, Sally, and Leo Cook; David Solomonov; and Danny Cook.

Artikim: The Art of Ice-Pops

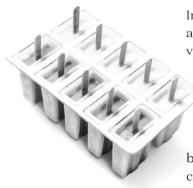

In many ways, Israel is a children's paradise. High population density and warm weather mean that life is lived outdoors, supported by a vast network of parks and a steady supply of ice cream. The dairy industry has been the pride and joy of Israel since its early days, providing a sustainable, calorie-rich, and economical food source. In recent decades, dairy has followed the standard Israeli playbook, leveraging agricultural technology to raise the world's most prolific cows. You'll see this legacy at an Israeli hotel breakfast, where a staggering variety is on display: yogurts, cottage cheeses, soft and aged cheeses from cow's, sheep's, and goat's milk.

Parents are rescued by Israel's ice cream, gelato, and frozen yogurt parlors, knowing how the mere prospect of a frozen treat can revive hot and cranky children. Maybe it's the sweetness of Israeli cream, the locally grown fruit that flavors it, or the blazing Mediterranean sun, but ice cream always tastes better in Israel.

We're partial to **Endomela**, the legendary chef Uri Buri's ice cream shop in the ancient northern port of Akko, where we tasted bracing mango and passion fruit sorbets, along with super-smooth ice creams in flavors like halva, date, mint, and cherry. **Buza** (Arabic for "ice cream"), a booming mini-chain founded by Adam Ziv and

Lemonnana

Makes 6 to 8

Lemon Verbena Syrup:
Combine 1 cup sugar and 1 cup water in a small saucepan. Bring to a simmer, stirring constantly, then immediately remove from the heat and stir in 6 sprigs lemon verbena or lemon thyme. Cool to room temperature, then refrigerate for at least 1 hour or up to overnight. Strain into a jar. Seal and keep refrigerated for up to 1 month.

Make the pops:
Combine ½ cup lemon juice, ¼ cup lemon verbena syrup, ½ cup corn syrup, 6 tablespoons water, 2 teaspoons sugar, ⅛ teaspoon kosher salt, and 24 mint leaves in a blender. Puree until smooth. Pour into ice-pop molds and freeze until firm, 8 to 12 hours.

Strawberry-Labneh

Makes 8 to 10

Combine 1 (16-ounce) container labneh, ¾ cup sugar, and ¼ teaspoon kosher salt in a food processor and process until smooth. Scrape into a bowl. Return 1 cup of the whipped labneh mixture to the food processor, add 5 ounces frozen strawberries, and pulse until the strawberries are evenly incorporated. Add this mixture to the whipped labneh and, using a rubber spatula, marble the two in a zigzag pattern. Spoon into ice-pop molds and freeze until firm, 8 to 12 hours.

Watermelon

Makes 6 to 8

Combine 1½ cups watermelon juice, 2 tablespoons lime juice, 1½ tablespoons honey, ½ teaspoon rose water, ¼ cup sugar, and ⅛ teaspoon kosher salt in a small saucepan. Bring to a simmer, whisking constantly, then remove from the heat and let cool to room temperature. Pour into ice-pop molds and freeze until firm, 8 to 12 hours.

Banana-Date

Makes 6 to 8

Soak about ⅓ cup pitted dates in hot water for 10 minutes. Drain and transfer to a food processor with 1 overripe banana, ⅓ cup sugar, ⅛ teaspoon kosher salt, and 2 tablespoons maple syrup. Process until the banana and dates are almost broken down (the mixture should be a little chunky). Add 1 (13-ounce) can coconut milk and 1 teaspoon lime juice and process until incorporated. Taste and add more lime juice, maple syrup, or sugar if needed. Spoon into ice-pop molds and freeze until firm, 8 to 12 hours.

The dairy industry has always been Israel's pride and joy, providing a sustainable, calorie-rich, and economical food source.

Alaa Sawatit, a Jew and an Arab, respectively, is another favorite. At their original Tarshiha location, in the north, we tried nearly a dozen flavors.

But it is the so-called novelty ice cream bars and ice-pops that are the most useful to frazzled parents and melting children. Their ubiquity is one of their best features: They're sold at storefront kiosks, by vendors with coolers trolling the beach, and at every park and tourist attraction in the country.

In Hebrew, *artik* is derived from the French word for Arctic and has become the generic term for ice-pops. Until the 1970s, the Artik company was the dominant producer of ice cream bars. With its sister company Kartiv, a leader in fruit-juice-based pops, Artik became to Israeli frozen treats what Kleenex is to facial tissue. There was even a popular children's song titled "Artik, Menta, Shokolad, Banana" (about mint, chocolate, and banana ice cream bars) that still plays in people's heads.

Ice-pops, or Popsicles (another brand name turned generic), are much easier to make at home than ice cream. Inexpensive molds are all you need for a kid-friendly project. And just like homemade gazoz, the results are far more wholesome. Sweetened fruit juices make great ice pops, whereas sweetened labneh mixed with fruit can become an ice cream bar. All our tehina shake mixes *(page 360)* can be frozen in ice-pop molds for a creamy, dairy-free treat. More fun: Dip the bars in melted chocolate and freeze for a few minutes to harden.

Ice-pops can be frozen for up to a month.

The Ice Cream Shop

Israel's warm climate, productive dairy industry, and kid-centric culture all happily conspire to make ice cream available around every corner. We love new-school shops like Buza *(above)* and Endomela *(left)* and old-fashioned places like Penguin *(opposite)*. And we dive into the inevitable slide-top freezer outside every storefront kiosk.

Acknowledgments

This is the third book that we have been privileged to write together, and with each one, we are more awed by the heroic efforts required of so many people.

To **Dorothy Kalins**, our partner, collaborator, and friend, this book is as much yours as it is ours. Your immense talent, insight, and experience (not to mention patience and persistence) were instrumental in telling this story. Your faith in us helped us find the confidence we needed to write this book. Thank you for having the vision to see where we were going even when we did not, and for keeping us on the right path when the road diverged (as it often did).

To **Don Morris**, our designer, for capturing the complexity of this story and making it look effortless. Your seamless weaving together of people, places, food, and words paints a picture that is beyond our wildest expectations. Thank you for your commitment to collaboration without compromising your point of view. Your generosity of spirit is all over these pages.

To **Mike Persico**, our photographer, we are thankful for the opportunity to see Israel through your eyes. There was no bus shelter too high for you to climb on top of, no sunrise too early to capture, no olive grove too fenced in to keep you out. Your talent and work ethic are matched only by your kindness.

To the brilliant **Rux Martin**, thank you for entrusting us with your imprint and for your support, encouragement, and thoughtfulness at every step along the way.

To our extraordinary publishing team at HMH: **Jamie Selzer**, there literally would not be a book without your kind and intelligent guidance; **Melissa Lotfy**, thank you for your good eyes; and **Sarah Kwak**, for always being there. And to **Elizabeth Herr**, for keeping us honest.

To **David Black**, our dealmaker, fixer, therapist, cheerleader, and oracle, thank you for helping to set this book in motion and keeping it on course.

To **Peggy Paul Casella**, for making our recipes accessible and doable, editing them, testing them, and making them better and more cookable along the way.

To **Avihai Tsabari**, our guide in all ways, and the whole team at your travel company, **Via Sabra**, for making the world of Israel our oyster (or kosher equivalent).

To the late, great **Gil Marks** and the indefatigable **Joan Nathan**, for their relentless and inspiring pursuit of Jewish food to the four corners of the earth, and for sharing the riches they brought back.

To **our children, David and Lucas Solomonov and Leo, Sally, Eva, and Danny Cook**, for inspiring us to be our best selves, letting us know when we fall short, and showing up for the odd photograph.

To **Gia Vecchio**, for your support, patience, and love.

To **Shira Rudavsky**, for your gentle but no-holds-barred first look at the words on these pages.

To **Adeena Sussman**, **Ronit Vered**, **Amit Aaronsohn**, **Osama Dalal**, and **Roger Sherman**, for generously sharing your time, expertise, and insights with us and for your work in putting a spotlight on the beauty of Israeli cuisine.

To **our colleagues at Zahav, Federal Donuts, Dizengoff, Abe Fisher, Rooster Soup, and Goldie**, we are honored to work with you and proud to have helped set something in motion that is so much bigger than us. It is truly humbling to watch you go to work each day. A special shout-out to **Dani Mulholland**, **Jilian Crosby**, and **Castianeira Jackson**, for deploying your intelligence, dedication, and creativity to keep us continually moving forward.

To **Andrew Henshaw**, for spearheading the recipe development and helping us make the food on these pages (often more than once). Special thanks to **our partners Caitlin McMillan, Okan Yazici, Brian Kane, Yehuda Sichel, Tom Henneman, Matt Fein, and Brien Murphy**, for enriching this book, our restaurants, and our lives.

To **the staff and residents of Society Hill Towers**, thank you for giving Zahav a home for the last ten years (and hopefully at least ten more).

To **the city of Philadelphia and our customers**, who enable us to do what we love to do every day. And to **our guests at Zahav**, who fill our dining room each night with warmth and joy.

We never tire of this
view from Jaffa of the
glittery city of Tel Aviv,
as it wraps around the
Mediterranean.

Index

NOTE: Page references in *italics* indicate photographs.

Index

Index

H

HaBoreeka (Carmel Market), 289

Haj Kahil (Jaffa), 89, 99, 115, 179

HaKosem (Tel Aviv), 67, 74, 89

HaKosem-style fried eggplant, 74, *75*

Halil (Ramla), 159

halva, 363

HaMalabiya (Tel Aviv), 330, 331

hamantaschen, 340, *340*

haminados, 77, *77*

harif (hot sauce):
    buying, 17
    and dates, pan-roasted
        turnips with, 172, *172*
    recipe for, 151

harissa:
    black (black garlic chile
        sauce), 150
    buying, 17
    fermented, 150
    fresh (North African pepper
        sauce), *69*, 150
    peanut, 150
    peanut, avocado with, 155,
        155
    tehina, 35, *37*
    in tehina ketchup, 35
    in Tunisian-style grilled
        tuna, 283, *283*

HaShomer (Carmel Market), 109

Hatzot (Jerusalem), 122–25

hawaij:
    making your own, 17
    spice blend, 150

hazelnut(s):
    dukkah, 173, *173*
    halva, 363

Hebrew phonetics, note about, 17

Helman Bakery (Jerusalem), 326

Henshaw, Andrew, 240

herbs:
    and Israeli salad, Goldie
        falafel with, *44*, 45
    see also specific herbs

horseradish:
    Abe Fisher beet salad, 190,
        190
    carrot chrain, 196, *196*

hummus:
    about, 140–43
    5-minute, with quick tehina
        sauce, 145–47, *146*
    serving as a meal, 152

Hummus Ben Sira (Jerusalem), 23

Hummus El Abed Abu Hamid (Akko), 169

hummus toppings:
    avocado with peanut
        harissa, 155, *155*
    black-eyed peas, 167, *167*
    braised cabbage with amba,
        167, *167*
    broccoli and pine nut pesto,
        166, *166*
    carrots and dukkah, 162, *162*
    charred asparagus with
        hazelnut dukkah, 173, *173*
    charred zucchini with mint,
        165, *165*
    corn salad, 157, *157*
    crispy oyster mushrooms,
        164, *164*
    ground beef with Turkish
        coffee, 170, *170*
    ground chicken with amba,
        160, *160*
    Japanese eggplant with
        muhammara, 161, *161*
    lamb meatballs, 170, *170*
    lima beans with tomato and
        cinnamon, 160, *160*
    matbucha with egg, 157, *157*
    pan-roasted and pickled
        eggplant, 171, *171*
    pan-roasted green beans,
        171, *171*
    pan-roasted turnips with
        dates and harif, 172, *172*
    pickled beets with
        pistachios, 164, *164*
    roasted butternut squash,
        156, *156*
    roasted corn with long hots,
        163, *163*
    saffron-braised chicken,
        154, *154*
    salt-roasted kohlrabi with
        garlic chips, 161, *161*
    tehina chicken salad, 154,
        154

I

ice-pops:
    banana-date, 365, *365*
    in Israel, 364–66
    lemonnana, 365, *365*
    strawberry-labneh, 365,
        365
    watermelon, 365, *365*

ingredients
    resources for, 17
    substituting, note about, 17

Itzik and Ruti (Tel Aviv), 206, 354

Itzik HaGadol (Jaffa), 179, 183

Index

Index

Index

Index